THE
FRENCH
REVOLUTION

THE LANDMARK LIBRARY

Chapters in the History of Civilization

The Landmark Library is a record of the achievements of humankind
from the late Stone Age to the present day. Each volume in the series
is devoted to a crucial theme in the history of civilization, and offers
a concise and authoritative text accompanied by a generous
complement of images. Contributing authors to The Landmark
Library are chosen for their ability to combine
scholarship with a flair for communicating their
specialist knowledge to a wider,
non-specialist readership.

THE FRENCH REVOLUTION

A Peasants' Revolt

DAVID ANDRESS

HEAD
of ZEUS

An Apollo Book

This is an Apollo book, first published in the
UK in 2019 by Head of Zeus Ltd

1 3 5 7 9 10 8 6 4 2

A CIP catalogue record for this book is available
from the British Library.

ISBN (HB) 9781788540070
ISBN (E) 9781788540063

Designed by Isambard Thomas
Printed and bound in Spain by Graficas Estella

Head of Zeus Ltd
First Floor East
5–8 Hardwick Street
London EC1R 4RG

WWW.HEADOFZEUS.COM

previous pages
Jules Girardet, *The Rebels of Fouesnant
Returned to Quimper* by the National Guard in
1792

PICTURE CREDITS
pp.6–7 Alamy Images; p.15 Gallica;
p.19 Public domain; pp.22–3 Christie's Images /
Bridgeman Images; pp.28–9 Public domain;
p.36 akg-images / Erich Lessing; p.39 Public
domain; pp.52–3 Bibliothèque Nationale /
Bridgeman Images; pp.56–7 Château de
Versailles / Bridgeman Images; p.58 Musée
Carnavalet / Bridgeman Images; pp.62–3
Musée Carnavalet / Bridgeman Images;
pp.70–1 akg-images; pp.78–9 Musée
Carnavalet / Bridgeman Images; p.81 Granger /
Bridgeman Images; p.88–89 Musée Carnavalet
/ Bridgeman Images; p.96 Library of Congress;
p.101 Universal History Archive / UIG /
Bridgeman Images; p.104 Library of Congress;
p.109 Library of Congress; pp.110–11 Musée
Carnavalet / Bridgeman Images; pp.114–15
Bridgeman Images; pp.128–9 Musée
Carnavalet / Bridgeman Images; p.130
Bibliotheque Nationale / Bridgeman Images;
pp.132–3 Public domain; pp.136–7 Musée
Carnavalet / akg-images; pp.148–9
Bibliothèque Municipale de Dinan /Bridgeman
Images; pp.150–1 Selva / Bridgeman Images;
pp.154–5 Musée Carnavalet / Bridgeman
Images. pp.156–7 DeAgostini Picture Library /
Bridgeman Images. pp.160 Public Domain;
pp.172–3 Public domain; p.177 Public domain;
p.179 Alamy images; pp.182–3 Christie's Images
/ Bridgeman Images; p.186 Library of
Congress; pp.198–9 Château de Versailles /
Bridgeman Images

Introduction

On 12 July 1789, as Parisians were launching an insurrection that would stun the civilized world, the English writer Arthur Young was travelling alone to the east of the capital, on the road between Verdun and Metz. Engaged on a tour dedicated to exposing and critiquing the shortcomings of French agronomy, particularly in comparison to Britain, Young filled the daily journal he kept with scathing observations on the poverty of the land around him, and the folly and ignorance of its people.

Walking his horse up a hill between the villages of Les Islettes and Mars-la-Tour, he fell into a conversation that was to become a staple of historical accounts, for by its timing and content it was almost too perfect. A 'poor woman, who complained of the times, and that it was a sad country' gave him details of the burdens her family's farm had to support, in taxes, tithes and other dues, and provided Young with the opportunity for some sententious commentary:

> This woman, at no great distance might have been taken for sixty or seventy, her figure was so bent, and her face so furrowed and hardened by labour, – but she said she was only twenty-eight. An Englishman who has not travelled, cannot imagine the figure made by infinitely the greater part of the countrywomen in France; it speaks, at the first sight, hard and severe labour: I am inclined to think, that they work harder than the men, and this, united with the more miserable labour of bringing a new race of slaves into the world, destroys absolutely all symmetry of person and every feminine appearance. To what are we to attribute this difference in the manners of the lower people in the two kingdoms? TO GOVERNMENT.[1]

The woman's words that Young recorded before this judgement are those which seemed to have the greatest prophetic quality: 'It was said, at present, *that something was to be done by some great folks for such poor ones, but she did not know who nor how*, but God send us better, *for the taxes and the dues are crushing us.*'

Recorded two days before the storming of the Bastille, these words seem to reach out of history as a plaintive plea from the masses, imprisoned in misery, crying out to be liberated. But they are, in themselves, more extraordinary than that. They imply, perhaps disingenuously – spoken after all to a mysterious foreign stranger – an ignorance of the ferment that had filled the countryside since the previous winter, a passivity wholly at odds with events taking place across France, and a deference that was quite the opposite of the way peasant communities were literally taking up arms to free themselves from their crushing burdens.

A few months previously, the inhabitants of Rouffy, a village further west near the regional capital of Chalons, had put in writing their demands for, among other things, new and fairly apportioned property taxes, the abolition of taxation on goods, the eradication of abuses in public administration, the institution of free justice, and for priests who took money from the tithe to be obliged to use it properly to maintain their churches and the 'ornaments, books, fabrics and sacred vessels, and to give alms in proportion to their tithes'.[2]

At the same time, the villagers of Achain, a day's ride southeast of Metz, had set out their demands, including this categorical claim:

> All those rights having their origin in the painful times of the
> feudal regime, when lords imposed on their subjects any yoke
> that pleased them, can be considered as true abuses, we request
> their reform: the province of Lorraine, being joined to France,
> asks to enjoy all the same privileges as the French, and to be free.[3]

Dozens of other villages within a few days' travel had made similar claims, hundreds within each province, several tens of thousands across the country. The landscape that Arthur Young rode across, bemoaning at each halt its lethargy and backwardness, was already breeding a revolution.

*

There is something uniquely scornful about the English word *peasant*. It has become detached from the root that still clings visibly to the French *paysan* or the Italian *paesano* – a person of the *pays*, the country; a local, or even, in the Italian version, a compatriot. The Spanish *campesino* points to a tiller of the fields, as do the old German terms *Landsmann* and *Ackermann*, while *Bauer* has come to mean 'farmer' in an entirely modern sense. The historical movement that Arthur Young embodied is one reason for the particularly negative associations that cling to the English term.

A true peasantry, in the sense of communities living largely from their own lands, lacking any strong dependency on wider market relations, had been fading from the English countryside for over a century by the late 1700s. Agricultural improvement took many forms, but always circled around the creation of larger farms, controlled by landlords seeking a cash profit from higher yields for sale into urban markets, eradicating the customary ways of the rural community in favour of deploying labour under expert orders. In the minds of people like Young, this was unequivocally how one brought an entire society to higher levels of prosperity, unshackling the productive potential of the population to do other things besides feed themselves. Those who would seek to resist such universally beneficial change could only be mired in the past, uncivilized, perhaps even scarcely human: peasants!

From such a perspective, where only the cutting edge of progress really matters, the fact that over two-thirds of the French in 1789 were actual *paysans* working the land (and 80 per cent of the whole population was, one way or another, embedded in rural communities), or that French countryfolk had succeeded across the previous seventy years in increasing production to feed a population that had risen by a third, appears to mean little. And it is not only in the minds of scornful contemporary Englishmen that this is so. The French revolutionary elites themselves were conscious of their own aversion to the *paysan*, and promoted the word *cultivateur* as a more politically correct label. While they used that label as if it restored dignity to the downtrodden, many of them seem to have understood agricultural communities as little more than a receptacle for superficial idealism.

The perennial cry of the revolutionary elite, faced by problems of urban unemployment, was 'Send them back to the land!' The height of the social radicalism reached by the leaders of Jacobinism during the 'Terror' of 1793–4 was to propose in the Ventôse Decrees the seizure of traitors' lands and their redistribution to 'poor patriots' – such people being assumed, unthinkingly, to want to be consigned to a small farm, and to know what to do when they got there. When in later years of conservative reaction a conspiratorial group of ultra-radicals plotted a coup d'état, their contribution to the history of socialism was the assertion that, after their revolution, landed property would be held in common. Thus, presumably, these first communists would have expropriated even the 'poor patriots' of 1794 (had there been any, which there were not, for both of these famous initiatives achieved precisely nothing).

History has paid far more attention to the authors of the Ventôse Decrees and the Conspiracy of the Equals than it has to the millions of French peasants who were the first to rise up in 1789, and the most ardent in defending a new revolutionary settlement in their favour: even, sometimes, against revolutionary leaders. Those peasants would emerge from a decade of turmoil emancipated by their own hands, even after being persecuted and reviled by radicals for not blindly following their lead, and sometimes driven into the arms of counter-revolution by the bigotry of urban elites.

The French Revolution was at its heart a peasant revolution, and as a peasant revolution it succeeded in benefiting far more people, in more far-reaching ways, than the revolution of lawyerly elites and urban so-called *sans-culottes* radicals that has dominated our impression of it. Those furthest from the centre rarely get their fair share of the light, and can even find their own words, like those of Young's peasant woman, turned to their condemnation. This book will show that we can witness the lives of the country people of the 1780s and 1790s, experience the complexity of their struggles, and respect the ways of life they fought for, in all their flawed human complexity.

The guillotine, a 'painless' means of execution that became
a totem of radical revolutionary violence.

The Peasants' World

It is hard to form a mental picture of how peasants lived several hundred years ago. To many observers, they seemed to be an undifferentiated mass, mired in what Karl Marx later dubbed 'the idiocy of rural life', standing out only as raw materials for the kind of reforms that would impose modernity on them. In truth, peasant households and communities are difficult to picture for the very opposite reason: the multiplicity of different individual and collective legal, social and economic arrangements they lived in, the turbulent changes to their lives over time, and their ever-resourceful efforts to fight back against the massive pressures perpetually bearing down upon them.

To picture a 'typical' peasant is already to take liberties with this kaleidoscopic pattern, but there are some valid things to be said. Firstly, one cannot pick out an isolated individual: although men were legally dominant in this highly patriarchal society, women worked alongside them in forming and managing the households around which all activity flowed. Both sexes pursued marriage as a vital economic strategy to which both were expected to contribute – inherited land, accumulated savings, family resources as dowry. Life was dangerous, and often brutally short: to reach marriageable age was already to be a survivor, something fully half of children born into the poorer classes did not achieve.

From the outside, peasant life might appear static, but as it was lived, it was a constant battle against time. Parents needed children to secure their own long-term future; each child was a dangerous pregnancy, each living offspring an ongoing battle against disease and hunger to reach an age at which they ceased to be an absolute economic burden and could begin working for their keep. Some peasant boys might scrape a little schooling from the village priest – girls almost never – but unless they showed peculiar promise what beckoned by adolescence was being put out to labour as a farm servant, cowherd or field hand, or for the girls similar more indoor work.

A servant-girl, the common experience of hundreds of thousands of adolescents, and the backbone of the lifestyles of the wealthy. (*The Kitchen Maid*, Jean-Baptiste-Siméon Chardin, 1738).

Life in their teens and early twenties was a further race, to build up a cushion of savings while awaiting the impact of chance and fate on possible inheritances (if their family owned any land at all), or an opportunity to take over a tenancy from an ailing parent. It was also a race against raging hormones, with marriage impossible until financial stability was achieved – averaging in the late twenties – and many couples finally going to the altar with their first child well on the way. The hope of the older generation was always that such matches represented a good bargain for the families' fortunes, and not just the regrettable outcome of a village dance, or something grimmer.

Thus the next generation could plant their household island in the fast-flowing stream, and hope it would last long enough for a robust family to take shape. Often it did not – pregnancies, accidents and diseases all cut back life expectancy – and a significant proportion of peasant families re-formed around second marriages, throwing step-children and half-siblings into the divisive and essential picture of looming inheritance. Families and communities adapted to such life-cycle shocks, as they worked constantly to manage their straightforward, grinding dependency on the cycle of the seasons, with all its ever-present risks and calamities.

Educated reformers were always certain that the peasantry could be taught to farm better, but this often involved imagining they could gain access to resources – better seed varieties, more sources of fertilizer, entire new crops – that were simply out of reach. Grim financial necessity held many peasants down to reproducing what previous generations had done. This was often allied to complex local conditions in other ways. The royal government fostered moves throughout the later eighteenth century to take areas of 'waste' land into production, which was possible in some areas, but could be blocked in others by the rights of landlords, and elsewhere risked – with the extra taxes and dues that would fall on new cultivation – costing the peasants more than it would produce.

Meanwhile in the prevailing conditions of the time, not even the most advanced agricultural practice was secure against pests and diseases, just as not even today is farming secure against extreme weather events. All of these could devastate individual fields, whole villages, even whole regions. On 13 July 1788, a massive hailstorm severely damaged ripening cereal crops across a significant swathe of central France, contributing to real shortages in the harsh winter that followed, and thus to the revolutionary situation of the following year. Against such threats, it is little wonder that communities clung to the possibility of divine intervention, with priests regularly offering up prayers for the harvest, and the ringing of the church bells to ward off thunderstorms a widespread practice.

All of the realities of their environment pressed down upon the rural population. Some rose, perhaps over generations of good reproductive luck and canny management, to landholding prosperity – from where, with some further investments of cash and time in education, a new generation might make the leap to the middling classes, and one day even beyond. But vast numbers of others could never take the first steps in that direction. One in ten of the whole population lived in destitution. While, again, bad luck accounted for some of this, much of it was due to the fact that society as a whole quite deliberately piled further burdens upon the peasantry.

*

Like every other pre-modern society, eighteenth-century France was built on the backs of its peasant population in two fundamental ways. Firstly, and essentially, everyone else depended on them to provide the food they ate. Such dependency, all too often transformed under conditions of poor weather and inadequate

overleaf
A nineteenth-century artistic vision of peasant life, caught between idealisation and recognition of the grinding labour involved.
(*Ploughing the Fields*, Eugène Alexis Girardet, 1877).

transport into fears of scarcity, stimulated not gratitude but resentment among the urban minority. Condemned to anxiously awaiting news of food reaching its markets, the population of the towns frequently resorted to disorderly protest, dreaded by higher authorities as a potentially calamitous loss of control. The long-term result of this was a highly regulated food-market system, in which the interests of the concentrated minority of urban consumers in stability of supply outweighed those of the conveniently dispersed majority of rural producers in maximizing income.

The attitudes that underpinned such choices were set in stone at the palace of Versailles, resplendent home of France's absolute monarchy since the 1680s. To the left of the main gates, paired with a figure of industry to the right, was (and is) an allegory of agriculture, a seated female figure surrounded by the products of fecund fields. She sits, literally, on the back of a man – the peasantry – depicted as a goggle-eyed gargoyle, mouth open in what contemporary artistic codes understood to be bestial lack of self-control, clutching a rag to wipe the sweat from his brow. The willingness to make such a depiction of France's economic dependence on the peasantry, in such a setting, reflects the second, and pervasive, way in which society battened on their labours.

The French social structure was driven by the concept of privilege: not as mere metaphor, but as real, legally enforceable distinctions. The more privilege a person could accumulate, the higher they had risen in the social scale, the less they owed to the state in taxes and other burdens, and the more they could demand of those below them. Inequality, and its oppressive consequences, was not merely an economic but a legal and political reality. Each aspect of this structure required, by its very nature, that there were losers. Without the unprivileged, privilege would not have been special. And the peasantry were the great unprivileged mass who bore the burdens of everyone else's distinctions. They paid, almost uniquely, the basic state tax on landed property, the *taille*, and the association between this burden and inferiority was such that 'taillable' was a label that in itself betokened social contempt.

State taxes, and the tithes demanded by the Catholic Church, were onerous burdens, and all too often marked with little evidence of a return for those who paid them. But they sat alongside a third pillar of exploitation, the system of seigneurial rights, that drove its divisive foundations even deeper into peasants' everyday experiences. A seigneur was a lord – the same word was used for 'Our Lord', God – and this was not a mere personal distinction, but a relationship of domination.

Once (so the story went) seigneurs had extended protection over their local villagers from their castle walls in unstable medieval times, receiving payments in return from people who were, over centuries, slowly liberated from being actual serfs, tied to the land by legal bonds. Tales of lordly generosity and paternal charitable care – *noblesse oblige* – permeated the historical memory of seigneurialism, blurring the changing landscape of several centuries into an indeterminate better olden days, against which the harsher realities of the late eighteenth century could be weighed, and found wanting. Seigneurs in the later 1700s might be the descendants of four or five centuries of nobility, but they might also be anyone who had accumulated a modest fortune and decided to buy into the lifestyle.

Seigneurial rights were legitimate property, traded on an open market. A package of documents changing hands in a notary's office could give a former wholesale merchant or lawyer the right to sit in the front pew of the local church, to have incense burnt in his honour, to charge a toll on the local bridge, to oblige farmers to pay to grind their grain at his mill or to bake their bread in his oven. And much more: to collect an annual share of every harvest; to divide and exploit former 'common' land; to plant or cut down trees; to maintain rabbit warrens and dovecotes, and have their inhabitants, and any other wild game, protected from attack when they ravaged crops; to charge any number of other minor or occasional dues; and to oversee the whole system with a seigneurial court, staffed by his own appointees, imposing penalties on any dissent.

Navigating all this, paying out as they went, was the peasantry's daily reality. In many places, seigneurial rights were leased, and sometimes further sublet, to businessmen whose only interest, therefore, was in screwing the maximum revenue from the system. In other places, a village might have its obligations split between several seigneurs, each materially little better off than the average villager, but still, in an entirely real sense, lording it over them.

*

Under all these burdens, in a multitude of different ecological zones and regional economies, agriculture supported communities with a strong sense of their own identity and place in the world. Isolated sheep-herding settlements in the high Pyrenees, villages bound to the slow rhythms of forest management in the Jura, vine growers along the slopes of the major river-valleys, stock-rearers and dairy-farmers, poulterers and market gardeners on the doorsteps of towns, and a whole spectrum of localities growing the precious staple grains that fed the whole population, all nourished their own peculiarities, and any scraps of legal privilege that fell down the social cascade, and might make their lives marginally easier.

Every hamlet large enough to have a church had the basis of communal life – somewhere to hold discussions after mass, and a cleric to read instructions, requests or admonitions from distant authority. Most villages had a formal legal identity as communities, and a set of elected or nominated male householders to represent them to the outside world – even if, often, appointed only with the seigneur's agreement.

Villagers lived within complex networks of economic and social differentiation and solidarity. Peasants actually owned somewhere over 40 per cent of all land, with households often combining control of small plots with rental of other lands to make a viable enterprise. Some regions were given over substantially to sharecropping, a system of rental where a large proportion of harvests was made over in advance to landlords. Near Paris, more advanced practices had taken hold, producing farms in concentrated ownership and large numbers of landless labourers. In some areas, landlords actually preferred peasants to retain ownership of small plots, because it tied them down and enabled lower wage rates and higher rents to be charged.

In many regions, work in cottage industries, producing goods that might eventually end up exported across Europe, or the world, supplemented incomes – while also producing the poisoned chalice of increased dependence on distant demands and merchants' investments. By the 1780s, burgeoning global growth in cotton had spread spinning wheels and looms far across rural northern France, but elsewhere similar woollen trades had long been embedded, as was silk weaving in some parts of the southeast. Local and regional specialisms in lace making, woodwork and leather goods also filled up time between farming tasks, and produced vital goods for sale.

Villages were compelled by the business of agriculture to some forms of solidarity. Hiring gangs of itinerant labour to help with harvests, for example, was a collective affair, as was the pursuit of legal claims against neighbouring communities when flocks strayed or boundaries fell into dispute. Much land use was governed by complex and variable sets of customary rights, sometimes over land actually held as communal commons, and sometimes where rights of gleaning, stubble grazing or pasturing

overleaf
An urban customs-house, living symbol of the burdens of
taxation and its intrusion into everyday life and commerce.
(*The Interior of a Douane*, Nicolas-Bernard Lépicié, 1775).

of flocks, or gathering of firewood and other resources, restricted usage of lands that were privately owned.

The kinds of dispute that might bring a village together against its neighbours could, within such a mesh of critical mutual obligations, rumble on inside any community as well. Common rights needed to be protected against misuse in a situation where every household was straining to make ends meet, and could be tempted to push their luck. The limits of solidarity could be drawn very tightly. Young men of the village might shout its name in defiance as they brawled with others at regional fairs, but householders looked askance at rowdy troublemakers the rest of the year, and eagerly denounced any 'sturdy beggars' to the overstretched royal highways police to be rounded up and locked away.

It was often noted that most of the peasantry were illiterate, and it was also true that the vast majority of them spoke local dialects, or entirely different languages (Basque, Breton, Catalan) rather than French. State officials and enlightened reformers pointed to this as a barrier to development, but such attitudes were themselves emblematic of the top-down desire to manage peasant lives for other people's notions of their own good. Reformers also sought to correct the tangled complexity of France's judicial and administrative systems, where layer upon layer of power and authority had built up over centuries, new systems too often merely supplementing rather than replacing old ones, and the boundaries of local jurisdictions ran chaotically and almost unmappably around and through communities and regions.

A group of neighbouring villages could easily find themselves beholden to networks of three or four different legal, judicial and administrative authorities, with no logic as to which communities fell on which side of which boundaries. But what looked like chaos to an outsider was, to those whose lives were rooted there, a landscape of possibilities. Every village was positioned in a web of legal and institutional relationships that was highly individual to its locality. Finding ways to play these against one another for maximum benefit was a vital survival strategy.

By the later eighteenth century, communities were increasingly adept at using royal justice provided by district courts to challenge the impositions of local seigneurial justice. Royal officials were keen to assert the superiority of their offices, and villagers faced increasing pressures to pay rising, and sometimes invented, dues to profit-maximizing seigneurs. Clever lawyers on both sides could keep disputes going for years.

Willingness and ability to engage in such actions also demonstrates that village communities were not isolated in their particularity. If there was no such thing as a newspaper that reached them, there were pedlars of other kinds of publications that passed through regularly, news from travellers and gossip picked up on trips to regular markets, as well as the steady drift of official demands. Many of the most geographically isolated regions enjoyed a very literal interchange with the largest urban centres, as their menfolk migrated seasonally, or over longer periods, for work – the stonecutters of the upland Limousin, for example, were in great demand in Paris. In parallel, domestic service swept up hundreds of thousands of teenage peasant girls into the world of the propertied classes, where most would stay for only a decade or so, saving up their dowry to make a respectable return to village or small-town life. The poor knew how the other half lived, because they had very often been part of the machinery of that lifestyle.

The Peasants' Voice

The peculiarities of every village's situation were abruptly made part of a grand national crisis in late 1788. The absolutist monarchical state, after decades of attempted reforms, had finally reached a decisive impasse in its efforts to modernize its chaotic, privilege-riddled taxation systems, and thus begin to pay off the mountain of debt accumulated in a series of global wars since the 1740s. Privilege, the legal condition that held down the peasantry, was both the underlying problem, and also the cause of active opposition to any change that might diminish the influence and social standing of powerful noble elites: 'absolutism' in practice was far from the exercise of absolute authority.

Desperate to find an overarching structure that would persuade the political nation to accept reform, the government gave in to the demands of its opponents to call an Estates-General – a national consultative assembly, rooted in medieval notions of a corporate society, that had not met since 1614. The time-honoured pattern for summoning such a body involved both local elections – which were decreed on a remarkably broad taxpayer franchise – and the specific formulation of grievances – *doléances* – to be presented as an agenda for the collective national consultation. The implication had always been, and was particularly present now, that such grievances, by being aired officially, would be noted and acted upon.

Thus, after having been studiously ignored in decades of rising Enlightenment debate about the character of the nation and the significance of public opinion, the peasantry was now called to rediscover its identity as the bedrock of the Third Estate – historically positioned behind the First, the Catholic clergy, and the Second, the nobility, but now destined, as one noted author put it in January 1789, to become 'everything'.

In that month, and the weeks that followed, literally hundreds of thousands, and possibly several million, villagers took part directly in meetings that opened up their whole world to questioning. Activist reformers from the middle and upper classes circulated written suggestions and 'models' for the *doléances* to be put forward, but the record shows that villagers, while they sometimes took note of these, also adapted them, adding their own concerns, or more often writing simply from their own perspective, digging deep into their personal and collective experience of abuse and oppression to demand that almost everything about the social structure around them should change.

They did so in ways that were often both respectful and uncompromising. The villagers of Bonnac in the foothills of the Pyrenees opened their document by addressing 'our very humble and very respectful thanks to His Majesty for having convened... his faithful subjects... in a way which is both constitutional and truly representative'. Here and in many other villages, *doléances* took care to spell out in detail the economic and geographical circumstances of a community, and the reasons why, from their perspective, change was necessary. At the same time, many reinforced this with assertions of willingness to work loyally in the interests of king and kingdom alike, 'until our last breath', as Barrineuf, not far from Bonnac, put it.[4]

State taxation was at the top of the vast agenda the country's *doléances* mapped out, because it was the proximate cause of the crisis, and was roundly denounced for its iniquities and complex injustices. Demands for a single uniform land tax, imposed without the massive exemptions enjoyed by the privileged, resounded from the four corners of the kingdom. So too did a clamour against the harsh and inefficient practice of 'farming' taxes out to private contractors, who gained quasi-state powers to pursue the population with unchallengeable demands, backed up by their own paramilitary forces. This was particularly iniquitous when used to enforce the infamous salt tax, the *gabelle*, which was charged at different rates in neighbouring regions, giving

A contemporary cartoon, depicting the literally crushing burden of taxation, borne by the unprivileged to support the privileged clergy and nobility. (Musée Carnavalet)

rise to an endless war between armed *gabelous* and smugglers.

From Salmonville-la-Rivière near Rouen came an epic denunciation of tax farmers 'and all the satellites in their pay. They are the leeches of the state, an all-devouring species of vermin, an infestation of plague.' The king was beseeched 'to so extirpate the roots of this pernicious plant, that it shall never regrow'. The peasants of Gastines in Bas-Anjou reported that, were they to accumulate even a little benefit from fattening a pig for themselves, 'three or four agents of the *gabelle* arrive, sworn enemies of the human race, who search, seize and plunder'.[5]

The ways in which physical boundaries – bridges, city walls – were used to impose multiple excise duties on goods moving through were also denounced, as again were the ways the privileged could simply declare themselves and their property exempt from such payments. Since tackling tax had already dragged the issue of privilege to the centre of attention, peasants did not hold back in assailing the abuses of the seigneurial system. They rarely dared denounce the idea of seigneurial status itself, but the abuses it occasioned – from courts that were supposed to give justice, but only served lordly self-interest, to bailiffs and agents who battened on the population, to the many ways of reimagining and reasserting rights to extort further revenue – were all condemned.

The villagers of Saint-Vincent-Rive d'Olt, just outside the southern town of Cahors, lamented that 'our community has so many charges to which it is subjected by a dozen seigneurs who have these rights recognized as easily as one changes a shirt'.[6] The inhabitants of Penguily on the north coast of Brittany spelled out in phonetic French their clear perspective: 'demandon que les labureure iret aux moullin ou bon leure sanbleret': we ask that farmers can go to the mill where it pleases them, and not be bound by seigneurial privilege.[7]

General demands for the end of privilege in taxation pointed implicitly to a radically different conception of the link between social status and the state. A few communities even dared articulate this more explicitly. Lignères-la-Doucelle in western Normandy asked that nobility in future become a reward granted 'only to those who have merited it'.[8] From Lauris, near Aix-en-Provence, came a denunciation of noble privilege as a condition robbing the nation of the benefits of emulation, since most could never aspire to reach its heights, and 'to thus deprive a state of the genius that might enlighten, instruct and defend it, is a crime'.[9]

The clergy, too, came in for some broadsides. The Catholic hierarchy was in many ways a microcosm of France, with many near-penniless priests serving isolated communities, while wealthy abbeys and convents dotted town and countryside alike, and appointments as bishops were monopolized by the nobility. While the clergy as individuals were sworn to poverty, many of them visibly lived a life of affluence, offering very little by way of spiritual services in return. Such was the complex interlacing of church institutions with other forms of privilege that it was far from unknown for an abbey to own the right to tithes on parishes many miles distant, to rent out lands it owned in other communities, and to be the titular seigneur of yet other places, gathering in revenues on all sides. Saint-Vincent again commented on their situation, forced to pay dues towards a religious hospital across the local river in Luzech, which did not actually take in any of their people, while they were barred from receiving aid from the larger hospital in Cahors.

The failure of such revenues to flow back to communities often in dire need of charitable support was vehemently critiqued in many *cahiers de doléances*, as the collected complaints were called. However, when the *cahiers* were gathered up and reviewed at the level of the some 300 district-court jurisdictions, where delegates met to elect their representatives to attend the Estates-General, much of the specific nature of village complaints was

Front page of the *cahier de doléances* of the parish of Méobecq, in the modern department of the Indre, with the 'destruction of the gabelle', the infamous salt-tax, highlighted as their first request.

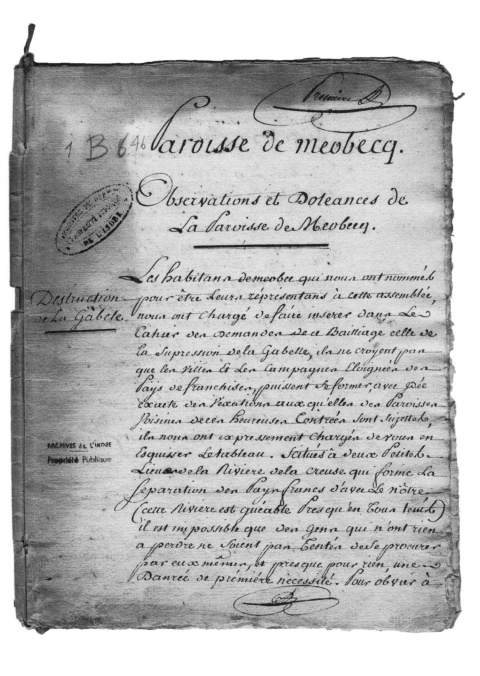

Parvisse de meobecq.

Observations et Doleances de
La Parvisse de Meobecq.

Les habitans de meobecq qui nous ont nommés
pour être leurs répresentans à cette assemblée,
nous ont chargé de faire inserer dans le
Cahier des Demandes de ce Bailliage celle de
la Supression de la Gabelle, ils ne croyent pas
que les villes & les Campagnes Eloignées des
Pays de franchise, puissent Se former, avec idée
exacte des vexations aux quelles des Parvisses
Voisins deces heureuses Contrées Sont Sujettes,
ils nous ont expressement Chargés de vous en
Esquisser Letableau. Scitués à deux Petites
Lieues de la Rivière de la Creuse qui forme La
Separation des Pays francs d'avec le nôtre,
(cette Rivière est guéable presqu'en tous tems,)
il est impossible que des gens qui n'ont rien
a perdre ne Soyent pas tentés de se procurer
par eux mêmes, et presque pour rien, une
Danrée de première necessité. Pour obvyer à

lost. Overshadowed by middle-class tendencies to focus on what were perceived as more important national issues of continuing representation and constitutional change, village concerns were easy to downplay as grumbling about pigeons and rabbits, hedges and ditch digging. The *cahiers* carried forward to Versailles smothered the peasants' voice under the concerns of a literate and propertied public.

*

By the time that the *cahiers* were drafted, it was already clear that the political crisis of the nation was colliding with an economic disaster. An exceptionally harsh winter had set in from November 1788, compounding the fragility of a country that had suffered a run of poor harvests in recent years (even before the devastating hailstorm of July 1788), and where trade had suffered a sharp downturn through two years of rumbling political crisis. Snowbound roads and ice-bound rivers prevented the transport of dwindling stocks of grain; animals deprived of fodder weakened; far into the south of the country frosts killed vines and olive groves. Government tottering on the edge of bankruptcy cold not act decisively to augment supplies, and the terrible threat of famine that hung over every pre-modern society loomed large as week after frostbound week passed.

In village after village across the country, peasant families, households and communities surveyed their situation, discussed and acted. Before the *cahiers* had been written, there had already been troubles – in Normandy the previous year, local officials had been denouncing each other for hoarding grain, terrified of a popular outburst, and wagon drivers had refused to carry the precious foodstuff between towns, for fear of mob attacks. By the start of 1789, the country around Besançon, for example, was full of rumours of a general rising against the oppression of the seigneurs, and over the next two months similar alarms appeared further south, first around Grenoble, then in Provence. The concern with such lords' abusive rights combined with the material fact that their granaries, like the tithe barns of the church, were packed with inaccessible food, taken from farmers' fields the previous year.

On 14 March, at Manosque, north of Marseille, a local bishop was stoned by a crowd that accused him of being a grain hoarder. Rioting convulsed the region in the following month. One bishop's palace was stormed, and the documents of his feudal and seigneurial rights seized and destroyed. Monasteries, seigneurial chateaux, mills and lawyers' offices were all likewise attacked. Communities pursued a twin-track policy of demanding the return of crops previously surrendered and seeking to destroy the documentary evidence of the underpinning seigneurial rights.

The village of Avançon, for example, in the mountains near Grenoble, first warned their seigneur in writing that they considered themselves free of his rights, then on 19 April demanded back from him the previous year's payments in kind. The following day they marched to his chateau to enforce this demand, searching the building unsuccessfully for the paperwork (and destroying nothing else), and left, issuing a one-week deadline for him to yield. An expedition of mounted police discouraged them from any further action, but the seigneur himself wrote to the national authorities, lamenting that his power in the community was now a dead letter.

Peasants themselves also wrote to Versailles, assailing ministers with complaints that urban and middle-class agendas had packed out the *cahiers*, and demanding support for their punitive and redistributive actions. The rumour that they did in fact have royal approval – in its most developed form, that there were 'Golden Letters' from the king authorizing an end to feudalism – circulated widely. It may have been a naive belief for some, but for others it was certainly a useful tactical shield.

As the weather warmed into spring, the food situation worsened. From Easter to August was always the hardest time of year, the *soudure*, when the fruits of the previous harvest aged and dwindled. With so little available to start with, prices spiralled and popular action grew more intense. In the far north of the country, large expeditions of peasants seized monastic grain supplies in April and May, progressing the following month to stocks held by seigneurs and even prosperous commoners, and adding in the forced renunciation of seigneurial rights.

By then, areas around Paris had seen months of activity by rural communities against the game reserves of the aristocratic elite – both desperately needed firewood and game on the hoof were stripped out, even from the queen's own private forests – and similar patterns were reported to the east, in Champagne. Grain riots convulsed Normandy and Brittany; the countryside around Lyon refused en masse to pay tithes; from Nîmes, Poitiers, Carcassonne and many other corners of the country food rioting, refusal of feudal payments, attacks on records and direct and violent challenges to authority of all kinds stirred the country towards a frenzy of fear and agitation.

*

Rural anxieties and actions were often shared by townsfolk: rioting in urban marketplaces against elevated grain prices had run through the towns of northern France in the early spring, flared up in Normandy and been part of the wave of unrest that struck the Marseille region. Townsmen's *cahiers* were just as ardent on the abuses of taxation and privilege as any village's. Yet fundamental divides remained. Peasants took action against those who 'hoarded' grain as part of a perceived process of moving it out of producer communities towards demanding and profitable urban markets, near or distant. Urban crowds descended on marketplaces to take action as overcharged consumers, demanding that grains be delivered to them at a 'just price'. In practice there were many places where these perspectives overlapped, where villagers needed to purchase in marketplaces too, especially where growing rural populations increasingly relied on cottage industry and the cash economy to survive. But the basic polarity remained, colouring attitudes in this crisis as it would in the years ahead.

Hints in some rural *cahiers* of resentment towards urban incomers – 'valets of independent means who assume the honourable title of *bourgeois de Paris* and let or buy a manor', as one parish in the Seine valley put it – were matched in many of the composite *cahiers* of the electoral districts by stark and scornful middle-class attacks on the rural poor. 'An elite of paupers that begins by begging and ends by stealing', characterized by a 'spirit of disorder, of independence, of roguery, of rapine and theft', were feared to be at large, and *cahier* after *cahier* called for sterner measures to crack down on idleness, drinking and the very concept of physical mobility for the 'dangerous' poor.[10] Longstanding antipathies about the lurking violence of the peasantry were boiling to the surface, driven by the grim reality of a crisis that had doubled the normal rate of indigence, leaving one in five of the population destitute and desperate.

Later in the summer, a local state official in central Brittany summed up the situation in the countryside that was causing 'me and all other sensible folk' to 'greatly fear' for the future. Peasants were reportedly determined to refuse all new tithe payments, 'and say quite openly that there will be no collection without bloodshed', declaring the tithes to have been abolished because such a demand was stated in the *cahiers*.[11] Other communities widely took this attitude to feudal and state exactions as well, and from the perspective of urban leaderships, a total breakdown of good order, with a concomitant real threat to property, had become a terrifying possibility.

A taste of that threat had erupted in April from the urban lower orders, in Paris itself. The teeming city of some three-quarters of a million people had its Estates-General elections delayed by several months because of security concerns, and when they did get underway, some ill-judged remarks from a wealthy manufacturer, taken to imply that a general wage cut might be imposed, sparked mass protest. Thousands of working people marched through the eastern districts of the city, clashing repeatedly with the military garrison, chanting slogans that identified themselves with the Third Estate, and eventually putting the factory of the imprudent speaker, Jean-Baptiste Réveillon, under siege.

Although the targets of the crowd's wrath fled successfully, the whole site was devastated, and troops were unleashed on the rioters with a ferocity that demonstrated the alarm they had provoked. At least several dozen people were killed, and reports elevated this to a possible several hundred. The judicial authorities swiftly hanged a handful of poor men, declaring them to be the guilty parties, and thereafter hoped they had suppressed any further tendency to unrest.

These 'Réveillon riots', that made dramatic national news just as deputies to the Estates-General were readying themselves to assemble at Versailles, helped to reinforce an emergent counter-tendency to the nationwide disorder. A year earlier, the city of Troyes had pioneered the introduction of armed volunteer patrols by members of its reliable propertied population to keep order where royal authorities were failing. Through the spring of 1789 other towns – Bar-sur-Aube, Sens, Amiens – followed suit. Still others – Étampes, Caen, Orléans – dusted off their statutes that allowed for official local militias, and re-formed companies of 'musketeers' or 'archers' neglected for decades. Marseille and Limoux combined the approaches, instituting semi-official militias without historical precedent. In several regions, urban and rural leaderships combined to form networks of armed men ready to defend property.

All such people understood themselves as 'patriots' rallying to a national crisis, and as spring turned to summer would increasingly understand that crisis as one provoked from above by the enmity of 'aristocrats'. Nevertheless, the immediate targets of their fears and aggression remained very often the poorer sections of the rural population, and France headed into the decisive weeks of what was to be a revolutionary explosion with the sharp edge of this social antagonism very much on display.

Crisis and Revolution

To understand how the continuing grievances and assertions of the peasantry contributed to the world-shaking phenomenon of 'the French Revolution', we must stand back and consider more broadly how the situation they confronted had come about. The origins of the Revolution unfolded as a series of nested crises, in which at each stage larger and larger groups, assumed by the protagonists of the previous level of crisis to be merely passive spectators, stepped forward to manifest their own concerns, articulate their own wishes and expand the scope of the problem.

Looking back to the 1760s, when the long-term problem of war debt occasioned many attempted reforms, the dispute appeared to be between the king's government and the elite of the judicial hierarchy. Ministers, appointed to enact the royal 'absolutist' will, clashed with noble judges who declared themselves defenders of a historic constitution, and thus entitled to oppose tax reforms that threatened structures of privilege. When the old king Louis XV, in the sixth decade of his rule and tired of arguments, closed down the judges' tribunals, the *parlements*, in the early 1770s, he seemed to be acting in the spirit of forward-looking 'enlightened absolutism'.

But the judges' rhetoric had played well with the wider educated reading public that was now to be found among the kingdom's propertied classes, increasingly active and interacting in the social and intellectual institutions of the Enlightenment. A vociferous pamphleteering 'public opinion' defied blanket censorship to condemn the abolition as an unconstitutional, anti-national coup, and when the new young king, Louis XVI, ascended the throne in 1774, he restored the *parlements* to their full powers, claiming explicitly to want to follow the infallible voice of that opinion. Ironically, over the next two years the new king's ambitious backing of an unimpeachably 'enlightened' minister, Turgot, led only to floundering and policy disasters, as conservative forces in the *parlements* and elsewhere discredited his moves towards economic liberalization. Turgot's subsequent fall was helped by a violent wave of grain riots unleashed across the Parisian region by a removal of market controls, which were rapidly reinstated as a result.

The monarchy played up to 'public opinion' by embarking on initially covert, then overt, financial and military support for United States independence. A new war against the old 'English' enemy proved highly popular, and the republican virtues of the new American nation, embodied in the canny figure of Ben Franklin, wooed curiously enthusiastic commitment from the aristocratic officer class. Through the later 1770s and early 1780s, the government avoided further crisis by relying heavily on loans and traditional temporary wartime taxes to fund military and naval efforts. But when a high-level political squabble pushed the energetic finance minister Jacques Necker out of government, his successors found themselves facing a completely unsustainable situation.

The debt burden had ballooned to the point where even attempting to service it over the long term without major reforms would collapse the finances of the state. Several years of peace from 1783, bringing urgent political demands to relax taxation, brought no solutions. By 1786, facing further recalcitrance from the *parlements*, Louis XVI and his minister Calonne agreed to bypass them with a device plucked from the history of the 1600s: an Assembly of Notables, a handpicked body of the wider social and political elite whose agreement to royal reforms would legitimize imposing them over *parlementaire* resistance.

As in previous waves of crisis, the Notables failed to deliver the passive acquiescence authority demanded. Meeting from February 1787, they denounced the debt situation as a product of ministerial incompetence, and reforms as a threat to the constitutional prerogatives of the privileged. Sent home after several months, having cost Calonne his job, the Notables left the monarchy once again battling the *parlements* over short-term expedients. Both sides increasingly appealed to 'public opinion' and the 'nation', with ministers issuing dire threats that they might throw their opponents to the people as if to the wolves.

Events accelerated further in the late spring of 1788, when the *parlements* were abolished for a second time, and a wave of unrest followed that went beyond the pamphleteering of the 1770s into major rioting. In August 1788, almost literally devoid of funds, the crown gave in and restored the *parlements*, permitting some desperate short-term borrowing. It was now that the idea of an Estates-General became unavoidable. It symbolically embodied an end to the 'absolutist' model of government, through a historical return to what was incautiously understood as a more open, consultative form of national rule.

The fact that such gatherings had been highly intermittent in the past, usually brief and often linked to crises, was overlooked. First mooted seriously by leading opposition voices in the Notables, and gestured towards as something that might happen in four or five years' time, by the summer of 1788 a meeting of the Estates in the following year had come to seem like the only salvation of a nation in collapse. But how was a body that last met in 1614 to be composed? The judges of the Paris *parlement*, guardians of constitutional rectitude, pronounced in September 1788 the only logical answer from their perspective: it would meet as it had last done, in three chambers, clergy, nobility and 'Third Estate', and each of the three would have equal voting weight.

This was the death knell of the judges' political relevance, as the enlightened public opinion they had earlier seemed to champion realized that such a backward-looking view of reality would condemn the vast majority of the public to passive marginalization. Outflanked by royal relaxation of censorship on the question of the Estates' composition, the judges were buried under a wave of articles, pamphlets and books proclaiming that the Third Estate was the real Nation, and merited a decisive voice in proceedings.

With the whole elite now facing the evidence of a wide movement of public mobilization, they continued to fudge the question. By the end of the year ministers had grudgingly agreed that Third Estate representation could be doubled, but whether to allow votes to be counted 'by head', and give real meaning to the doubling, had been abandoned to the future decision of the Estates themselves. As the government, under the recalled wonder worker Necker, juggled short-term financial expedients, it issued remarkably relaxed instructions for the holding of elections and the drafting of the *cahiers de doléances*. Royal authority continued to believe that the people would fall into line behind its agenda, while the educated men who thought they led public opinion likewise convinced themselves that the country at large would fall into line behind them.

The country by the end of 1788, suffering through a near-famine winter, was no longer minded to passively follow anyone, and through both the *cahiers* and direct action, made that emphatically, dangerously, clear in the coming months. Through these same months another political force also began to gather strength, as the nobility was forced to face up to the idea that its natural, God-given social superiority, embodied as an assumption in all the elite resistance of previous years, was actually under threat not from royal despotism, but from the despised commoners of the kingdom.

*

Until the crisis around the Estates-General erupted, French nobles surveying their social world would have had many reasons to assume that the status they enjoyed was a universal aspiration. The lawyers and merchants who poured their life savings into land and feudal rights as soon as they could were all aiming, so

overleaf
A depiction of the ceremonious opening of the 1789 Estates-General, produced for its first anniversary, when France's course towards a constitutional monarchy still seemed relatively smooth. (Bibliothèque nationale de France)

OUVERTURE DES

à Versailles,

Ainsi fut convoqué sous le meilleur des Rois,

Ce Sénat des Français, ce Tribunal suprême,

Présentée et Dédiée

Le 4 Mai 1790.

Cette Salle a été construite par Mr. Paris, Chevalier ...

ÉTATS GÉNÉRAUX
le 5 Mai 1789.
Qui, soumettant aux Loix l'orgueil du Diadème,
Détrôna les abus, et nous rendit nos droits. *Palissot*

à l'Assemblée Nationnale ?

Par Helman, Graveur de Madame.

Gravé par Helman, de l'Académie des Arts de Lille en Flandre.

Helm. du Roi, Dessinateur ordinaire du Cabinet de sa Majesté.

et chez M. Ponce, Graveur Rue S. Hyacinthe N° 19.

it appeared, towards the blessed goal of *vivant noblement*, living nobly untroubled by the cares of business, and thus able to devote themselves to higher things. Across the country, nobles graced the institutions of enlightened sociability that had spread far and wide in previous decades. Both official academies of learning and unofficial local literary circles joined groups such as agricultural improvement societies in fostering civilized and reforming exchanges. Meanwhile, in a more sordid recognition of the benefits of their status, the marketplace for costly royal offices, that could be bought and sold just as feudal rights could, saw soaring prices in the 1780s as owners of new wealth from burgeoning global trade sought the noble status such transactions offered.

The electoral process disrupted all of this. One key reason was that it opened a sudden chasm between those who were actually, legally, noble and those merely *vivant noblement* on their way up the social ladder. Anyone without the necessary documentation was cast down to vote with the rabble of the Third Estate, and many impoverished country squires and ex-army officers took great delight in rediscovering the power of certified ancestry against wealthy parvenus. This was further reinforced in the electoral process itself, as noble voters rejected almost entirely the claims to election of the ennobled class of royal office holders and judges. They sent to Versailles a body of men capped with some figures of genuine eminence – including the ardently reformist marquis de Lafayette – but largely comprised of men hostile to bourgeois social pretension, and increasingly alarmed by a flow of pro-national writing that quite clearly threatened the core of their social identity.

The Third Estate, meanwhile, was finding its voice as the nation. The several hundred district meetings that produced the final elected deputies had injected their composite *cahiers* with a clear agenda of urban and middle-class demands for permanent constitutional change and the end of fiscal (and implicitly other) privileges. This did not mean they sought any kind of austere levelling down. The Third Estate who came to Versailles in time for a grand opening session on 5 May 1789 was dominated by lawyers, many of whom were also landowners, and some of whom had been conspicuously *vivant noblement*. Official protocol demanded that they all wear a dowdy black costume for the ceremony, contrasting with vivid clerical robes and gold-adorned noble vestments. Legend has it that this became a badge of honour, but in truth over a third of the deputies simply refused to be thus sartorially downgraded, and a vote to adopt it as a uniform failed decisively.

What all the deputies found at Versailles, when the opening ceremonies were over, was a blank space where government ought to have been. With continued social unrest across the country, Necker and the king gave almost no lead, either on the organization of Estates business, or the agenda for discussion. Initially meeting in separate rooms, the three Estates became deadlocked over the preliminary question of verifying the electoral credentials of each deputy. Reformers pressed for this to be done jointly, paving the way to demand that business would be transacted by the whole Estates as one body, giving weight to the Third's doubled headcount. Conservatives in the nobility and clergy resisted, and for over a month none of the three chambers could be brought to a positive decision on anything.

These extraordinary conditions of aimless, yet increasingly tense, stagnation gave the Third Estate deputies, still gathering in their chamber every day, the chance to discover each other, to begin to experience the demands of speaking in an assembly, and to conduct what more than one referred to as a school of national identity and politics. Ideas that had begun to take shape in pamphlets over the previous year were clarified and promoted, and individuals with the firmest convictions about the situation began to come to the fore.

overleaf
The design of Jacques-Louis David's monumental canvas intended to celebrate the Tennis-Court Oath of 20 June 1789: never completed, because in the years ahead, so many of the participants became outcasts from revolutionary politics.

By mid-June, the Third Estate grasped the nettle, and voted by a large majority to declare itself the 'National Assembly', summoning the other two Estates to join it as a unified body and embark, not just on government-led reform, but on the writing of an entirely new modern constitution for France. This conviction was sealed on 20 June when, panicked by finding their chamber locked, the deputies adjourned to a nearly indoor tennis court and swore an oath to remain united and produce such a constitution, regardless of the dangers.

Their chamber had in fact been locked so that it could be redecorated for a formal session in the presence of the king on 23 June (such were the demands of court protocol). This previously unannounced initiative presented all three Estates, at last, with a royal reform plan – but one that, apart from taking away some fiscal privileges and gesturing towards more regular consultative assemblies, offered no acknowledgement of the idea of a National Assembly and a constitution. Ordered to go back to meeting as separate Estates, the National Assembly refused, as an increasing trickle of more reformist clergy and some nobles were joining them day by day. The king, on hearing of the refusal, did little more than shrug, but others around him were intent on more decisive action.

Country squires had not been the only ones who feared the claims of the nation. From the end of the previous year, the king's own brothers and cousins, the Princes of the Blood, had begun to argue forcefully that royal authority was under threat from the new political ideas of the reformers. By the end of June they were convinced, along with the queen herself and most of the royal family, that the monarchy faced an insurrectionary threat that had to be met with force. The deputies at Versailles needed to be cut off from potential support in Paris – where the garrison that had repressed rioters in April was now dangerously mutinous – and presented with a new government that would

The first stirrings of Parisian uprising on 12 July 1789, after news of Necker's ousting reached the city, depicted in one of an extensive series of contemporary illustrations by the Lesueur brothers. (Musée Carnavalet).

insist on submission to the 23 June agenda, or else. Louis XVI was harangued into agreement, with the added emotional blackmail of the safety of his children dangled before him. Military orders went out from the beginning of July, setting tens of thousands of troops in motion towards the capital, many of whom were from Swiss mercenary or otherwise 'foreign' regiments, seen as inherently more reliable in a crisis.

*

The court plotters struck on 11 July, royal orders dismissing Necker from office and installing a ministry of trustworthy conservatives. But from its first hours, the coup was mishandled. Not enough reliable troops were in position. Military leaders warned that they could not even guarantee to defend key locations in the capital. And the scale of popular response to the news of Necker's dismissal took them completely by surprise. Parisian crowds understood immediately what was happening, and linked it to soaring bread prices as part of a 'famine plot' to subjugate the

Premiere SCÈNE de la RÉVOLUTION Française A PARIS.
Le 12 Juillet 1789, on apprit à Paris que le Roi renvoyoit M.ʳ Neckre : Les Factieux qui n'attendoient qu'une occasion pour éclater saisir celle là , et firent agir leurs agents, les quels Suivis d'une foule de peuple qu'ils avoient ameuté parcoururent les divers quartiers de la Ville, excitant les citoyens à la révolte ; L'un d'eux montant sur une borne haranguoit le peuple, tenant les discours les plus séditieux ; On portoit les Bustes du Duc d'Orléans, et de M.ʳ Neckre ; l'après midi ils furent à tous les théâtres faire cesser les Spectacles.

population. Protest marches on 12 July led to clashes with troops, and overnight into attacks that destroyed many of the dozens of customs posts that hemmed in the city. Stocks of food were liberated from urban monasteries, but with members of local electoral assemblies and the turncoat garrison taking the lead, more indiscriminate looting was punished with summary execution. This was an insurrection, not a mere riot.

The city-wide assembly, created months before to elect Estates-General deputies, summoned into being a citizens' militia. An invasion of the Invalides arsenal produced thousands of muskets, but the city's stocks of gunpowder were locked inside the fortress of the Bastille. Thus, on 14 July, after several attempts at peaceful negotiation had failed, troops of the garrison and the militia, and crowds of local people, fought their way inside the medieval structure, suffering over 100 dead and crowning these events with legend.

One dimension of that legend was the brutal killing of the Bastille's governor, along with the city's royally appointed mayor, for acts deemed treacherous by the crowds celebrating their victory. Set against those killed in the storming, and against the potential deaths of a military attack on the city at large, such executions were almost insignificant. But as unpunished, and indeed celebrated, killings of distinguished figures by a common mob – and thus vile and unnatural occurrences to an elite mindset – they acquired totemic significance. So too did crowd killings of two other senior officials a week later, dragged from hiding and blamed specifically for the threat of the 'famine plot'.

By that time, the echoes of the Parisian uprising had begun to spread nationwide. They had run through the panicked National Assembly ever since 12 July, when it began a permanent session that came to feel like a siege, ever alert for the arrival of royal troops to arrest the deputies, and hearing of uproar in Paris with no idea of its meaning. When news arrived that the city had arisen for their protection, and triumphed, the eruption of tension and joy was such that one deputy reportedly succumbed to a stroke. When on 15 July the king himself arrived in their hall, almost unguarded, and declared himself (with very little choice) at one with them, there was further rejoicing. This was crowned with a celebration two days later in Paris, as the king was welcomed into the city by its self-appointed revolutionary leadership, and all declared themselves united to work for the common good.

Such gestures, however, merely guarded the National Assembly from immediate dissolution. The 11 July plot had proved to the satisfaction of all that there were real and dangerous enemies of reform. The king's own youngest brother, the comte d'Artois, had fled abroad, along with other actors in the plot, and made no secret of their intention to resist anything the Assembly attempted to create. A growing body of aristocratic emigration – the émigrés – was a reality from the summer of 1789, and so was the perception, often exaggerated but never entirely false, that their tentacular connections reached back disruptively into every corner of the nation.

At this moment the peasantry again made their presence felt in national politics, but as so often it would be through events poorly understood at the time, and later discounted as irrational and sub-political. Peasant communities that had engaged in all the various resistances and insurrections of the spring and early summer, and those that had merely heard news of them from other localities, stood primed to expect a backlash. Communities had long memories of earlier times when hunger or mistreatment had pushed them into direct action, and how there had always been a price to pay. From mid-July, sometimes influenced by news from Paris, but sometimes generated locally, the fear of an 'aristocratic' attack on the nation's harvests, using the swelling ranks of the suspiciously indigent as their 'brigand' agents, began to swirl across France.

Later generations would come to call this the 'Great Fear', and stress that no actual plot on this scale existed, but in the context of the events of preceding months, not only was it perfectly rational to expect such a danger, but both aristocratic and patriotic groupings in national politics would blame each other for stoking such alarms. Nobody was cool headed in these weeks. The Great Fear was the spreading of alarms from a half-dozen original incidents of mistaken identity or over-reaction, through specific local and regional routes of communication, to hundreds if not thousands of particular localities – in some cases, almost faster than seems possible.

Primed to expect and respond to such news, communities armed themselves and passed on the alert, before sometimes going on patrol (spreading further evidence of armed strangers), or undertaking the same kind of chateau invasions and requisitions already seen months earlier. In a context of the total collapse of state authority, all this was in fact a pragmatic, community-oriented response, and there is remarkably little evidence of wanton violence occurring. Two nobles were killed in a confrontation in the Norman village of Ballon, north of Le Mans, and a third in a clash at the other end of the country, at Pouzin in the Vivarais. But that is the sum total of deadly violence recorded for a wave of activity that swept the country. If anything, the Great Fear on the ground reinforced peasant communities' sense that a change had already taken place, and that they had a new role in standing up for themselves against the authorities that had overshadowed them for generations.

*

How this looked from the centre of politics was slightly different. News from the various regions, near and far, travelled to Paris and Versailles no faster than a mailcoach could carry it, with word from different places often assimilated en route.

A reality of multiple transitory alarms became the impression of waves of simultaneous national upheaval. Community mobilization, seen through the eyes of fearful property owners, translated into the threat of total dissolution of order. Since the traumas of mid-July, the National Assembly had found itself in an increasingly disturbing limbo. Royal authority had evaporated, although all agreed that the king remained the centrepiece of the constitutional order they desired. Royal government was paralysed. Necker had been three-quarters of the way into exile before he could be found and summoned back to resume his post at the end of July, and now had no policy initiatives to propose beyond a constant battle to scrape together enough cash to stave off bankruptcy.

Deputies combed the *cahiers* for inspiration, finding agreement on ending fiscal privileges and opening government up to a national legislature, but little else. Noble status, and particularly the rights of *seigneurs* over the general population, loomed large, but threatened a divisive struggle. In the first days of August, a cohort of more radically reformist deputies, including some nobles, who had begun meeting around the nucleus of a 'Breton Club' of Third Estate representatives from Brittany, began to push for a decisive intervention. Brittany had been particularly convulsed in recent years by recalcitrant noble opposition to reform – so much so that its aristocratic provincial institutions boycotted the Estates-General. With this behind them, the commoner Breton deputies were willing to strike out at the very structure of privilege itself.

With their encouragement, in an Assembly session on the evening of 4 August, two reformist noblemen, the vicomte de Noailles and the duc d'Aiguillon, almost fell over each other to propose the ending of seigneurial rights as a dramatic break in the current logjam. Other speakers followed, from both the nobility and the clergy, prompted by a combustible mixture of fear at the situation around them and the heady fumes of Enlightenment virtue, kindling a verbal conflagration of privilege that lasted into the small hours of the morning.

One observer called it 'a kind of magic' as defenders of privilege like the duc du Châtelet cast away their collected penumbra of powers and entitlements. A more cynical observer might note that du Châtelet was one of the commanders of the Paris garrison until resigning on 16 July, and might have well-founded fears of a grim fate unless seen to side with the people. He also insisted that he expected a 'just compensation' for giving up valuable rights, and stepped up a second time to demand an end to the church tithe, just after a clergyman had put seigneurial hunting monopolies on to the metaphorical bonfire.[12]

Another observer spoke perhaps more tartly of a 'combat of generosity' between different groups, that also saw the Breton Third Estate deputies take a lead in renouncing the provincial privileges that their noble brethren treasured so much. There were already limits and hesitations coming into effect. Contemporaneous records indicate that, after midnight, motions for full religious liberty, the abolition of nobility as a concept, and the suppression of colonial slavery had garnered applause. But none of these three appeared in the hastily written list of sixteen key areas that was voted through by acclamation before the session finally closed. One commoner deputy wrote home in the immediate aftermath that 'we are a nation of brothers. The King is our father and France is our mother.'[13] Such fraternal joy, however, barely survived the arrival of daylight.

Over the following days, the Assembly's elected secretaries drew up a fair copy of the resolutions, and they came forward for a confirming vote on 11 August. News of what had happened on the 'Night of 4 August' had already spread around the country, of course, helping to calm some of the more immediate agitation. As deputies began to feel the immediate crisis slackening, they began to take a more pragmatic approach to what had actually been given away.

The decree of 11 August boldly began with the declaration 'the National Assembly entirely destroys the feudal regime' – inventing a catch-all term for the range of privileges it was about to attack.[14] The second and third articles ended rights over the keeping and hunting of game, including specifically pigeons, reflecting how ardently these practices were detested, although a loophole was left for hunting reserves around Paris for 'the personal pleasures of the king'. Next the Assembly ended the existence of seigneurial courts 'without compensation', although insisting that their officers continue to perform their functions until replaced by a new system. Likewise, after a long article enumerating the various forms of tithe that were abolished, it ordered that they continue to be paid 'in accordance with the laws, and in the customary manner' until replaced by a new means of supporting the church.

This pattern ran through the whole document. The sale of royal offices was abolished, but the Assembly promised to reimburse the holders for their value, and asked them to continue their functions until replaced. Privilege in the matter of taxation, in the right to hold public offices, and the privileges of geographical entities, provinces and towns, were abolished outright. But the core of feudal privilege, the seigneurial dues that actually battened on the peasantry, were a different matter. Like royal offices, these were valuable property.

From its first article, the decree insisted on this distinction. Rights it associated to personal servitude and the relics of serfdom were abolished explicitly 'without compensation', but all others were declared 'redeemable', on terms to be set later by the Assembly, and, crucially, would 'continue to be collected until reimbursement has been completed'. This pattern was reiterated – the curious institution of feudal tithes, owned by bodies other than the church, 'will be redeemable', but meanwhile 'the National Assembly orders that their collection will also be continued'.

All 'perpetual rents on land' and all other harvest dues that made up the great bulk of the routine feudal burden were likewise redeemable – but only redeemable, and their owners were fully entitled to keep collecting them in the meantime. What it would mean to redeem this burden was not yet specified, but it was widely assumed that it would mean paying a lump sum of some twenty years' dues – treating them as if the annual payment was 5 per cent interest on invested capital.

This was not the change that peasants across the nation had been creating through a thousand acts of communal resistance for the past half a year. If villagers wanted to know what the National Assembly thought of their deeds, they had only to refer to a decree promulgated the previous day, which informed them that 'disorder and anarchy' spread by 'false alarms' were a 'criminal plan' conceived by the 'enemies of the nation' to prevent 'the establishment of liberty'.[15]

Here they would also learn that municipalities, militias and the regular army were ordered to co-operate to hunt down 'the leaders of these conspiracies' and subject them to 'exemplary punishments', and that 'all seditious gatherings… even under the pretext of hunting' were to be 'immediately dispersed' by the forces of the new order. Such authorities were also to compile registers of all 'disreputable persons, men without trade or occupation, and those with no fixed domicile'; all such persons were to be disarmed of any weapons, and kept under surveillance by the 'national militia'.

*

The French peasantry quietly digested the implications of the National Assembly's attitudes over the following months, weighing them against the hard fact on the ground that villagers had taken firm control of their own destinies in practice (and would be rewarded shortly with the consecration of each village as a formal 'municipality', entitled to elect a mayor and council to govern its affairs). The countryside relapsed into relative calm in the later months of 1789, as peasants turned to gathering their precious harvests, and quietly refusing to pay taxes, tithes and dues that most collectors were too prudent to insist upon. Meanwhile in the capital, the fears of the urban consumers, the self-interest of the propertied, and the dread of counter-revolution, all combined to stir up new decisive changes.

The National Assembly spent late August 1789 addressing the question of how to start a constitution, deciding that it needed to be prefaced by a Declaration of Rights, and then wrangling for several weeks about what to put in such a document. Deputies were chauvinistically insistent that it be a declaration with general import, proclaiming the superiority of French intentions to the whole world. Yet what they wrote was little more than a compendium of middle-class grievances against the way France had been governed, turned on their heads into general-sounding propositions. There were declared to be 'natural and imprescriptible' rights – but only four, 'liberty, property, security, and resistance to oppression'. Much of what followed hinged on defining 'the law' as the arbiter of the limitations of rights, emergent from a sovereignty which 'resides essentially in the Nation', and functioning as 'the expression of the general will'.[16]

In a telling juxtaposition, it was stated that only the law could define the conditions under which one could be 'accused, arrested or detained' – a blow at arbitrary executive authority – but equally anyone summoned by the law 'must obey at once', and 'renders himself culpable by resistance' – a very curious insertion into a document about rights. Freedoms of speech and opinion were guaranteed, but they must not 'trouble the public order established by the law', and 'the abuse of this liberty' was

Blue-coated National Guards and Parisian women celebrate their victory in the
October Days as they march back to the city - bearing green branches as symbols
of peace and triumph, but also the heads of two royal guards.
(Bibliothèque nationale de France).

noted as punishable 'in the cases determined by the law'. People's rights were very much to exist only within an authoritative, and potentially authoritarian, framework of positive legislation.

Most of the final third of the declaration was taken up with very specific propositions about the right to elect national representatives, and public oversight of government expenditure, before ending at Article XVII with the emphatic statement that private property, as 'an inviolable and sacred right' was safeguarded from state confiscation except in cases of 'public necessity', and then only on 'condition of a just and prior indemnity'. The class that had invested billions in feudal rights and state offices was carefully marking the need for them to be reimbursed, in this supposedly universal statement of values.

The Declaration of Rights, although widely publicized through unofficial channels, remained officially unpromulgated, as did the decree on the feudal regime. The king, as head of the government, was exercising an unofficial veto through inaction, just as the Assembly plunged into a bitter debate in September about whether to give him an official one in the new order. Radicals and conservatives had produced a remarkable united front on another matter, almost unanimously rejecting the idea of a legislative upper chamber (seen as a power grab by entitled reformist grandees). Debate on the veto swirled more aimlessly before coalescing around the notion of a 'suspensive' power that could block a new law, but be overturned by a later vote of two consecutive legislatures.

Outside the Assembly, in Versailles itself, other nearby towns and on the streets of Paris, a wave of popular agitation about the food supply, and economic disruption generally, was gathering speed. The new militia, now dubbed the National Guard, dealt swiftly with the demands of unemployed wage labourers in the capital: thousands were rounded up and shipped off to their home provinces. Public meetings of other working people demanding relief, and in some cases rights of political participation, were banned, but it proved much harder to block the time-honoured practice of female consumers protesting the price and scarcity of bread. From mid-September onwards there were intermittent protests, demonstrations and seizures of grain shipments. Twice, crowds surrounded the City Hall demanding redress.

Then came news that on the night of 2 October, the king and queen had hosted a banquet at Versailles for an arriving regiment of troops, at which 'counter-revolutionary' toasts had been offered, and the newly adopted tricolour cockade, sacred emblem of the Revolution, was allegedly trampled underfoot. A sudden fusion of alarm at this development in politics and the ongoing food crisis brought tens of thousands of both women and men onto the Parisian streets on 5 October, and by the afternoon their leading elements had decided to set off for Versailles, to seek redress from the heart of government. In a spectacular and complex collision of traditional female roles in provisioning crises, ceremonious petitioning and a sudden breakdown after dark into dangerous violence, this intervention radically shifted the course of the Revolution.

The marquis de Lafayette, appointed leader of the Parisian National Guard, persuaded Louis XVI that safety lay in yielding to a rising crowd demand for him to move to Paris. The people seem to have believed that having him there, with his family, half-hostage, half-guardian, would safeguard them from 'famine plot'. The parade back to the city that he accompanied the next day was a carnivalesque triumph. Ever after, however, Louis was to see himself as quite fully a prisoner, and with Queen Marie Antoinette, to begin to work ever more determinedly to reverse the Revolution. The National Assembly voted to follow the royal family to Paris, and established itself there in temporary quarters only days later. On 21 October, it voted into existence a new statute on martial law, to be used against any future public disorders.

Failures and Betrayals

While Paris settled into its new reality as the centre of government and politics, the country at large continued to stew in an unpalatable blend of old and new practices, vast unsettling changes and odd continuities, grand pronouncements and gritty local conflicts. Many seigneurs and their agents refused to give up hope of collecting their feudal entitlements from the 1789 harvest, and the final much-delayed promulgation, in November, of the decree on the feudal regime merely encouraged them, since the letter of the law was on their side.

Angry exchanges, mostly verbal but occasionally physical, began to flare up again nationwide as the winter drew in, and in the southwestern region of the Périgord grew into something much bigger. The experiences of the previous year translated into a dramatic willingness for communities to band together and assert their rights in a changed situation by force. Large groups of armed peasants began visiting local chateaux in December, demanding the return of collected dues, with varying degrees of aggression. The urge for community solidarity against further payment also sometimes took on a hard edge, with threats to hang 'the first to pay his rent' reported.[17]

When in January 1790 the authorities arrested several alleged ringleaders and imprisoned them in a local town, nearby villages raised a force of over 4,000 men, invaded the town, released the prisoners and threw a local notable into the cells instead. Over the next three months this resistance spiralled out across a wide region between Bordeaux and Montauban. Direct attacks on feudal dues were accompanied by the symbolic burning of seigneurs' church pews and the pulling down of weather vanes that only the privileged had been allowed to erect.

More than 300 communities were engaged in over 100 separate expeditions and incidents, commonly involving several hundred people at a time. A local practice of planting celebratory maypoles was taken up and given a revolutionary twist with tricolour decorations, producing the first examples of what would become a nationwide practice of planting 'trees of liberty' in the months and years ahead.

While such actions, with their mobilization for material self-interest, are relatively easy to assimilate to an idea of popular momentum carrying revolution towards the future, it would be wrong to make an artificial distinction between communities' sense of economic identity and their wider cultural roots. Scarcely had this regional movement begun to die down than southern France in general was shaken by a series of sectarian religious disturbances.

Huguenot Protestants remained a significant minority across the south, despite a century of persecution since Louis XIV revoked earlier measures of toleration. Fervently Catholic groups were enraged at the end of 1789 when civil rights were granted to these 'heretics', and one such group's leader met with the émigré comte d'Artois, resident in Turin and spreading promises of material and ideological support. While the nudge towards open conflict thus came from a quite specifically aristocratic and reactionary source, people in town and country alike proved to need very little encouragement to organize around religious identities. Rival Catholic and Protestant militias formed across southern France through the winter, and by early spring 1790, agitated by a failed effort in Paris to have Catholicism formally declared to still be the state religion, were primed for conflict.

Toulouse saw rioting at the end of April as pro-revolutionary crowds assailed Catholics who had gathered to petition for the rights of the church; in mid-May Montauban saw an insurrection of local Catholics, begun by a demonstration of several thousand women to stop the authorities inventorying religious property for sale. A new and effectively counter-revolutionary local government had to be disarmed through negotiation, as columns of

overleaf
A Lesueur illustration of the planting of a
liberty-tree, here in the form of an organised
civic festival in a town. (Musée Carnavalet).

Dans l'enthousiasme de cette Liberté que l'on croyait
s'être donné, on imagina de planter des arbres pour
en perpetuer la mémoire, ce qui ce fit dans chaque
section avec grand appareil, les Gardes nationaux
accompagnoient le Maire, et une Musique brillante
rendoit cette fête interessante.

National Guards from as far away as Bordeaux threatened to converge on the city.

Worse was to come. In Nîmes in the southeast, a Protestant merchant oligarchy had taken control of the town in elections. The fear of a heretical Huguenot takeover, abetted by Artois's counter-revolutionary urgings, produced shocking violence. Catholic forces rose against the local authorities in June, prompting appeals by both sides to their co-religionists in nearby villages, an influx of armed men, and a gruesomely bloody Protestant victory that became a massacre of around 200 Catholics, including a number of clergy.

The events that reached this lamentable peak sprang out of key contradictions emerging as the revolutionary settlement took shape. Some of these lay at the very heart of its project. The confluence of nation, sovereignty and 'general will' written into the Declaration of Rights marked something close to a metaphysical conviction among the National Assembly, and the wider political class, that there could, should, and must be unity, and essential unanimity, in political action.

Decisions the Assembly took in subsequent months – to have only one national legislative chamber, to bar members of that chamber from serving simultaneously as government ministers, to prohibit open candidacy for elections, demanding that electors nominate the 'best' men in the privacy of their own reflections – all pointed towards a conviction that the nation could only be dangerously divided by anything that looked like political partisanship, or the 'checks and balances' of a system that acknowledged the realities of competing perspectives and goals.

As the Assembly spread democratic elective forms outwards and downwards to the country at large, doing painstakingly detailed work to define what kinds of public office could be held simultaneously, or not, by individuals, how long they might serve, and what the duties of different roles were, they seem never to

The Declaration of the Rights of Man and the Citizen, a contemporary, and relatively plain, rendering of the iconic text, distributed by the Goujon music publishers of Paris.

DÉCLARATION

DES DROITS DE L'HOMME

ET DU CITOYEN,

Décrétés par l'Assemblée Nationale dans les Séances des 20, 21, 23, 24 et 26 août 1789, acceptés par le Roi.

PRÉAMBULE.

Les représentans du peuple François, constitués en assemblée nationale, considérant que l'ignorance, l'oubli ou le mépris des droits de l'homme sont les seules causes des malheurs publics et de la corruption des gouvernemens, ont résolu d'exposer, dans une déclaration solemnelle, les droits naturels, inalienables et sacrés de l'homme : afin que cette déclaration, constamment Présente à tous les membres du corps social, leur rappelle sans cesse leurs droits et leurs devoirs ; afin que les actes du pouvoir législatif et ceux du pouvoir exécutif, pouvant être à chaque instant comparés avec le but de toute institution politique, en soient plus respectés ; afin que les réclamations des citoyens, fondées desormais sur des principes simples et incontestables, tournent toujours au maintien de la constitution et du bonheur de tous.

En conséquence, l'assemblée nationale reconnoît et déclare, en présence et sous les auspices de l'Être suprême, les droits suivans de l'homme et du citoyen.

Article Premier.

Les hommes naissent et demeurent libres et égaux en droits; les distinctions sociales ne peuvent être fondées que sur l'utilité commune.

Art. II.

Le but de toute association politique est la conservation des droits naturels et imprescriptibles de l'homme; ces droits sont la liberté, la propriété, la sûreté, et la résistance à l'oppression.

Art. III.

Le principe de toute souveraineté réside essentiellement dans la nation : nul corps, nul individu ne peut exercer d'autorité qui n'en émane expressément.

Art. IV.

La liberté consiste à pouvoir faire tout ce qui ne nuit pas à autrui. Ainsi, l'exercice des droits naturels de chaque homme, n'a de bornes que celles qui assurent aux autres membres de la société la jouissance de ces mêmes droits; ces bornes ne peuvent être déterminées que par la loi.

Art. V.

La loi n'a le droit de défendre que les actions nuisibles à la société. Tout ce qui n'est pas défendu par la loi ne peut être empêché, et nul ne peut être contraint à faire ce qu'elle n'ordonne pas.

Art. VI.

La loi est l'expression de la volonté générale; tous les citoyens ont droit de concourir personnellement, ou par leurs représentans, à sa formation; elle doit être la même pour tous, soit qu'elle protege, soit qu'elle punisse. Tous les citoyens étant égaux à ses yeux, sont également admissibles à toutes dignités, places et emplois publics, selon leur capacité et sans autres distinctions que celles de leurs vertus et de leurs talens.

Art. VII.

Nul homme ne peut être accusé, arrêté, ni détenu que dans les cas déterminés par la loi, et selon les formes qu'elle a prescrites. Ceux qui sollicitent, expédient, exécutent ou font exécuter des ordres arbitraires, doivent être punis; mais tout citoyen appelé ou saisi en vertu de la loi, doit obéir à l'instant; il se rend coupable par la résistance.

Art. VIII.

La loi ne doit établir que des peines strictement et évidemment nécessaires, et nul ne peut être puni qu'en vertu d'une loi établie et promulguée antérieurement au délit, et légalement appliquée.

Art. IX.

Tout homme étant présumé innocent jusqu'à ce qu'il ait été déclaré coupable, s'il est jugé indispensable de l'arrêter, toute rigueur qui ne seroit pas nécessaire pour s'assurer de sa personne doit être sévérement réprimée par la loi.

Art. X.

Nul ne doit être inquiété pour ses opinions, mêmes religieuses, pourvu que leur manifestation ne trouble pas l'ordre public établi par la loi.

Art. XI.

La libre communication des pensées et des opinions est un des droits les plus précieux de l'homme : tout citoyen peut donc parler, écrire, imprimer librement : sauf à répondre de l'abus de cette liberté dans les cas déterminés par la loi.

Art. XII.

La garantie des droits de l'homme et du citoyen nécessite une force publique : cette force est donc instituée pour l'avantage de tous, et non pour l'utilité particuliere de ceux à qui elle est confiée.

Art. XIII.

Pour l'entretien de la force publique, et pour les dépenses d'administration, une contribution commune est indispensable : elle doit être également répartie entre tous les citoyens, en raison de leurs facultés.

Art. XIV.

Les citoyens ont le droit de constater par eux-mêmes ou par leurs représentans, la nécessité de la contribution publique, de la consentir librement, d'en suivre l'emploi, et d'en déterminer la quotité, l'assiette, le recouvrement et la durée.

Art. XV.

La société a le droit de demander compte à tout agent public de son administration.

Art. XVI.

Toute société, dans laquelle la garantie des droits n'est pas assurée, ni la séparation des pouvoirs déterminée, n'a point de constitution.

Art. XVII.

Les propriétés étant un droit inviolable et sacré, nul ne peut en être privé, si ce n'est lorsque la nécessité publique, légalement constatée, l'exige évidemment, et sous la condition d'une juste et préalable indemnité.

Se vend à Paris, chez Gouion, marchand de musique, grand'cour du Palais-royal où se trouve le Tableau de la Constitution faisant pendant à celui-ci.

have contemplated how to accommodate conflict into this system. They had reached agreement shortly after moving to Paris, with almost no discussion, that women, poor men, and other marginal groups could not be trusted with a vote that required robust independence to exercise it, but they seemed to believe that a national electorate of several million robustly independent men would reach a natural consensus on everything.

It was essentially an administrative, not a political, vision, that wiped the geographical slate clean of the chaotic mess of previous distinctions, and imposed a crisp map of new 'departments', subdivided equally neatly into districts, cantons and municipalities, with local government, judicial and even religious functions distributed by election. But none of this spoke to the issue that had emerged dramatically in Toulouse, Montauban, Nîmes and many other places – what to do if people sought, in practice, to contend for power.

The realities of life in both rural and urban communities before 1789 had produced a richly textured local political landscape of networks and factions, sometimes mere loose affiliations between households, sometimes arranged around rival religious fraternities or friendly societies, sometimes the followers of rival local power brokers, or real 'clans' of close and distant kin. Such rivalries might play out as anything between niggling conflict over precedence at local events, to manipulation of tax liabilities and court cases, to full-blown bloody vendetta. All of this, and the extent to which it inevitably carried over into the question of who took power in the new revolutionary order, was simply invisible to France's bold constitution makers.

This failure to see what politics on the ground actually was – to wilfully ignore, for example, that the map of new departments they had settled on was itself the product of months of intense and highly self-interested lobbying by the newly anointed local capitals (and their disappointed rivals) – carried over into sweeping assumptions about what all further dissent must actually be. There was no place in the National Assembly's vision for the concept that millions of people might legitimately begin to disagree with the course of the Revolution. In some senses, the idea of loyalty to the nation simply replaced the idea of loyalty to the king as an implicit guarantee of good conduct – as if decade after decade of internal strife among loyal monarchical subjects was not what had brought France to its revolutionary pass.

*

As the Revolution moved towards its first anniversary, discord continued to mount. Religious conflicts intensified as the National Assembly pressed on with the logical consequence of the abolition of the tithe, and a decision later in 1789 to effectively nationalize all church property and lands, creating *assignat* bonds based on their value to ease the state's debt crisis. Stripped of independent resources, the church was informed that its hierarchies were to be assimilated to the state, and treated as a public service, while its organization was rationalized: monasticism, unless directed towards education or healthcare, was abolished in February 1790.

It was the coolly logical move to inventory newly redundant monastic buildings for sale that prompted the riots in Montauban in May, and July 1790 saw the promulgation of a proposed Civil Constitution of the Clergy, setting in train the equally logical, but emotionally shattering, abolition of over a third of bishoprics and a significant number of parishes, as they were to be forcibly realigned with the new sets of civil boundaries. The king resisted signing this for months, demanding consultation with the pope, and escalating tensions further.

In village communities that had had their identity as self-governing municipalities affirmed mere months before, and elected their own mayors and officials sometimes only weeks previously, news like this struck a further blow at the idea that the politicians in the capital understood anything about their lives. Many communities had begun to keep their new municipal records with a clear sense that they were active contributors to a new political project, with a voice to be heard. When, for example, the village council of Saint-Pastour in the new Lot-et-Garonne department heard in March 1790 about plans to reorganize the judiciary, they expressed 'sorrow and surprise' at the apparent loss of the summary courts and highway police, exposing their community to 'evildoers, vagabonds and assassins'. The mayor was delegated to call a meeting to discuss what could be done – though the answer, of course, was nothing.[18]

Elections for successive waves of new administrative roles dragged out over the course of the next year and witnessed plummeting rates of participation, from what had been substantial majorities of male householders in many regions, down towards a fifth or even less of the 'active citizen' cohort. It would soon frequently be the case that only those with some personal stake, as an associate of an office holder, or otherwise some vested interest in the outcome, could be driven to engage in the long-winded polling process. Municipal registers, once the lively voice of newly empowered communities, dwindled in later years towards dull administrative records and, increasingly, a numbing rhetorical conformity.

Contributing to this disillusionment, peasants continued to reel from attacks on their economic situation. In mid-March 1790 the National Assembly had reaffirmed and tightened its position on the redemption of feudal dues, displaying a total lack of sympathy for those who bore their burden. Each peasant subject to dues had to go about redeeming them as an individual, barred from communal organization or agreements; each such peasant also had to redeem all the various dues owed to a former seigneur as a package (regardless of the practicality of meeting such costs), or not at all. Any seigneur, meanwhile, who might have difficulty after the events of 1789 in producing original documentation of his rights was allowed to use any evidence of having previously exercised them to make a valid claim.

The extent to which this clashed with peasant perceptions was clear in the letters of complaint that seigneurs regularly directed to the National Assembly. Two weeks after these decisions, the comte de Brancion wrote from Lorraine of the defiance of the village of Royaumeix. The inhabitants 'firmly believe that the intention of the National Assembly is that they need not pay any rent or seigneurial due, even those owing for 1789, and that they are permitted to shoot, at all times and everywhere, all types of pigeons belonging to former seigneurs'. The latter was, of course, strictly true, but the comte lamented that one local had taken it upon himself to massacre Brancion's birds 'before the eyes of my sisters and nephews', saying it was his right: 'This man belongs to the municipality.'[19]

Intransigence escalated on both sides. On 3 May the Assembly reiterated that its redemption policy had not been a mistake, and added final confirmation that cash dues had to be redeemed for twenty times their annual value, and dues paid in kind for twenty-five times that value, in cash. Occasional dues, such as for land transfers, had their own sliding scale of payments. Unredeemed dues were, once again, declared to be a permanent obligation, and a legally enforceable debt. There was no mechanism in the legislation to compel a seigneur to accept redemption, and presumably, if he did not, the obligation merely continued, for ever.

From many peasants' perspective, it was coming to seem as if the new authorities also intended to maintain other oppressive elements of the old order for ever. The village authorities of Marnay in the Haute-Saône found themselves writing to the National Assembly in April 1790 in a tone of near-incredulity after local judges had fined a man for fishing in a pond formerly subject to seigneurial privileges: 'In vain were the laws on this subject cited, the rights of property entreated; in spite of everything this judge condemned him to pay six livres and costs; all this proves quite obviously that this judge thinks the river still belongs to the former seigneurs.'[20]

From the central department of the Creuse, a petition to the Assembly lamented that its March decree had allowed seigneurs to 'recommence their old vexations'; from the Lot in the southwest came a complaint in June that seigneurs had put in a demand for the payment of arrears in kind, carefully timed as the cash price of grain peaked.[21] In the face of such a staggering repudiation of the peasant revolution of 1789, it is not surprising that some communities reacted with shock and disbelief. Tactics for resistance varied widely across the country: while some resorted to mulish resistance, other communities launched formal legal challenges – 69 of 129 municipalities in the far-southern Corbières region did so, for example.

Still others entered into niggling processes of detailed contestation, offering cash payments instead of in kind with one hand, threatening to refuse to move payment in kind to seigneurial barns on the other. The take-up of actual redemption was minuscule – of the 129 Corbières villages, only one did so, its seigneur receiving 11,555 *livres* payment for what had been an exceptional light package of burdens. Non-payment, on the other hand, was endemic, setting virtually the whole rural community at odds with what revolutionary authorities thought they should be doing.

The complexity and bitterness of dispute in individual villages again emerged in seigneurs' complaints. In early July 1790, the seigneur of the village of Garravet in the Gers, some 18 miles (30 km) southwest of Toulouse, wrote in apparent fear of his life. On 20 June the local mayor had announced to the whole village that he had received a decree 'which forbade the community to pay any dues and authorized them to seize the communal lands'; and a week later the seigneur's farms had been invaded, his fences torn down and his crops stolen:

> Since this event, several of them have had it said to me that they want to buy gunpowder to blow up my house; that I am forbidden to appear by day or night in Garravet; my men are forbidden to gather my harvest or thresh in the usual places; the priest is forbidden to see me or allow me to stay with him; all are forbidden to pay me any dues or to grind their grain at my mill, on pain of death.[22]

He had been threatened directly with violence, and the situation had only worsened after the mayor had admitted, a further week later, that he had no such decree. After the priest had read the Assembly's real decrees on the subject, the peasants 'replied, in a majority, that they did not need such authority, that they were the masters; in consequence, they have put their beasts in all my fields'.

In the complex and uncertain atmosphere of revolution, with written news and verbal rumour often hard to distinguish, the peasant tactic of simply asserting that what they wanted to happen was true – as with stories of royal orders for pillage in early 1789 – was widespread. Sicaire Linard, secretary of the municipality in the hamlet of Léguilhac de l'Auche in the Dordogne, was denounced to higher authorities in the summer of 1790 for announcing an imaginary decree banning payments by sharecroppers to their landlords. As in Garravet, threats of violence were also common. In another Dordogne village, the council's legal officer and National Guard drummer were denounced for stirring up a crowd to resist paying their taxes, and threatening that 'the first tax collector or syndic who came to ask for their payment, they would shoot him with a pistol'.[23] Both men were jailed as a result.

In the midst of this ongoing agitation, and mere days after the religious violence of the spring culminated in massacre at Nîmes, the National Assembly did what the counter-revolutionaries had feared for the past year, and formally abolished noble status itself, the use of noble titles, the display of coats of arms, and any other public acknowledgement of social hierarchy. The educated and propertied men running the Revolution continued to make a sharp distinction in their minds between the social and cultural panoply of the Old Regime – as it was increasingly called – and the economic structures that had

The spectacle of the Festival of Federation, which greatly enthused Parisians and the national middle classes, even if it did not penetrate far into the countryside. A painting by the contemporary artist Pierre-Antoine Demachy (Musée Carnavalet).

underpinned it. To the peasant victims of the system, this looked like attempting to demolish it with one hand while shoring up its worst effects with the other.

Unsurprisingly, the rural response was lukewarm when the national and Parisian authorities combined to organize a Festival of Federation for 14 July 1790, marked by a military parade and oath-taking ceremony in the capital that brought hundreds of thousands together, including tens of thousands of provincial National Guards. Those visitors were largely from the prosperous urban classes, who could afford to give themselves a political holiday amid the bustle of Parisian crowds.

Larger towns and cities had the time and resources to put on parallel subsidiary 'federations', and to treat the whole thing as

an expression of national unity. Many villages did not. At most perhaps half marked the occasion in some minimal form – there was, after all, a formal requirement for all local National Guard units to take the loyalty oath – but that left another half of communities doing nothing, out of indifference, or out of an anxious and rising hostility towards what the Revolution was actually turning out to be.

Just over a month after the 14 July festivities, more than 25,000 National Guardsmen and others gathered, under arms, at the chateau of Jalès in the Ardèche, about 30 miles (50 km) north of Nîmes. Properly authorized by the local department, this was nonetheless an essentially sectarian meeting. All present were ardent Catholics, come to protest the events of recent months and demand the release of their imprisoned co-religionists. Further demands to purge Protestants from local government in the region were acclaimed, though the leadership of local notables checked the rank-and-file calls for immediate militant action to that end.

Bringing together local peasants and townsmen, this gathering bound them into a semi-clandestine network that local authorities tried half-heartedly to disrupt at the National Assembly's urging. Their failure was marked by the wide distribution two months later of a manifesto from the 'Faithful Frenchmen, armed... for the cause of their religion and of monarchy against the usurpers of the so-called National Assembly', the start of a string of such provocative calls for a rising against a revolutionary leadership declared to be criminal traitors.[24]

As feudal and religious issues continued to dog the communities that had denounced them as burdens in the 1789 *cahiers*, so the end of 1790 saw renewed strife about the third critical component of the peasantry's complaints: state taxation. Having essentially ignored their existing obligations for the best part of two years, those who owned or worked land were stung with the abrupt consequences of the rationalization of fiscality. Indirect taxes, those on the movement of goods, were abolished, leaving a significant hole in the national balance sheet.

Without any effective means of inventorying urban property or invested wealth, the National Assembly went ahead with what had in fact been demanded in many *cahiers* – a single tax on all agricultural land, already conveniently registered. But such registers were of highly variable sophistication, and made wildly differing assumptions about the quality and productivity of land. If the peasantry in early 1789 had expected to be given a taxation system that relieved them of unfair burdens, they were sorely disappointed.

Thanks to the vagaries of documentation, some did well. In the Ariège, high in the Pyrenees, the new tax assessment barely reached 20 per cent of the levels experienced by peasants of similar wealth in the Seine-et-Marne near Paris. But the abolition of provincial privileges saw whole regions suddenly hit with taxation they had never contemplated paying before. Areas of Brittany saw their burden literally double as their blanket exemptions fell away, and a scattering of other regions across the country saw similar rises, with little rhyme or reason to their effects. A few lucky areas, such as the Puy-de-Dôme around Clermont-Ferrand, saw no great rise, but no expected fall either; the region of the Nord, around Lille, saw average assessment go up by only one-sixth, but the result was that they paid more than the Bretons even after the latter's doubled burden. Or rather, they were supposed to pay more.

The ground truth of the new tax system remained endemic refusal – less than half of what was nominally owed was collected in the first year of operations, and far less in subsequent ones. Some of that early relative success may have been due to the shock with which methods of collection hit local communities. It remained common for local authorities to auction off tax gathering as a profit-making opportunity: this of course put cash into the public coffers immediately, boosting the first year's returns, but also smacked of the iniquities of Old-Regime tax farming, and prompted further resistance from the actual taxpayers.

From late 1790 onwards, some urban-based authorities took the uncompromising line of mustering their National Guards and launching literal raids on villages to extort payment. This aroused horrifying echoes of the worst brutalities of the pre-revolutionary tax authorities, so central to the burdens denounced less than two years before. From near Carcassonne in the south, one village priest wrote to lament that communities of 'the most sincere friends of the constitution' were being attacked by militia behaving 'as if on enemy soil'. He noted that he was writing in place of his community's mayor, who had been dragged off into custody.[25]

Before the end of 1790, two further assaults on the peasantry's hopes began. The first was the coming together of the process for selling off the confiscated lands of the church – more than one-twentieth of all farmland – with that of compensating royal office holders for their lost positions. The National Assembly accorded over 800 million *livres* in new *assignat* bonds to this compensation (almost doubling the national debt in the process). As was the overall intention, many of those who received this windfall of capital poured it into the investment-grade agricultural property that had so fortuitously just hit the market (thus, in the tidy minds of the National Assembly, dissolving that portion of the national debt represented by the *assignats* handed over).

Sold by auction in large plots, these *biens nationaux* or 'national property' boosted the wealth of the already wealthy, while communities had to stand by and watch their best fields pass from the hands of one absentee landlord to another. The district of Cholet in the new Maine-et-Loire department, for example, saw over 56 per cent of all church lands sold to members of the bourgeoisie, and less than 10 per cent to working peasants.[26] This and neighbouring districts were at the heart of a western region becoming increasingly disaffected with the results of the Revolution as a whole.

To add insult to injury, the Assembly closed out the year with another piece of prejudiced economic logic. It declared that landowners with existing rental contracts were entitled to receive from their tenants the additional income that would have been paid in tithe on their fields, and in the south, where the old *taille* was assessed on each plot of land, the value of that as well. The argument was that landowners were now the liable taxpayer, and the state was entitled to draw through them on revenues previously paid by tenants – but in practice, of course, this was simply a new burden on such tenants, and a loss of any nominal gain from changes in the system.

It came on top of what was already a widely decried practice of landowners simply increasing rents with the assertion that abolished taxes and dues gave the peasantry more capacity to pay. Overall, in an economy where many peasants both owned and leased land, paying both taxes and rents, and where the new revolutionary landlord class were often exactly the same people as the Old-Regime seigneurial class, the question of what the Revolution had actually done for the peasantry, eighteen months on from the 'abolition of feudalism', remained disturbingly ambiguous.

Sliding to Disaster

The first weeks of 1791 saw yet another dramatic escalation in the Revolution's internal conflicts. Angered and mystified by the persistent refusal of the clergy to settle down into acceptance of their Civil Constitution, and deeply suspicious of possible counter-revolutionary tendencies, the National Assembly imposed a loyalty oath on all priests, to be taken publicly at a Sunday service before their congregations. Failure to do so would by default strip a cleric of his official position.

With the Catholic hierarchy still awaiting papal guidance, and the king's conscience known to be deeply troubled, it was a defining moment. Almost every French bishop refused the oath, aligning the upper ranks of the church decisively with defiance of the revolutionary order. Across the nation, around half of all priests likewise refused – some point-blank, with expressions of anger and defiance, some regretfully, some trying to offer modified 'oaths' that salved their consciences over the collision of the spiritual and the secular. At a stroke, tens of thousands of clergy became opponents of the new order, and thousands of communities were decisively disrupted.

Le Déménagement du Clergé
J'ai perdu mes Bénéfices rien n'égale ma douleur

Oath-refusing ('non-juring' or refractory conduct) formed a distinct geographical pattern. In every region there were some who fell on both sides of the issue. In a large quadrilateral in the centre of the country, from Bordeaux to Dijon, the Ardennes to Dieppe, in general well over half of priests took the oath; this was also the case in regions bordering the Alps, and scattered portions of the southwest. Elsewhere – up and down the Rhône valley and westwards into the neighbouring highlands; along the western shores of the Rhine, and the northern border provinces; and above all in a dozen departments of western Normandy, Brittany and the lower Loire valley – a majority of all priests were refractory. In some areas, such as the Moselle in the east and the Vendée in the west, three-quarters of all priests refused.

Congregations reacted in a wide variety of ways to this conduct. In Paris, which saw an almost even split in its local clergy, a population kept on high alert by repeated rumours and an inflammatory press was soon hounding refractory priests and their supporters as counter-revolutionaries. In other towns, and even some villages, any non-juror risked the same response: incidents of priests being physically attacked after, or even during, the service in which they declined the oath were reported around the country.

Some communities denounced their non-juror to the authorities with long accounts of his previous iniquities, so that revolutionary loyalties and local vendettas became hard to untangle. On the other hand, some non-jurors spoke with regret of a break due entirely to their personal spiritual conscience, and were regretted by patriot communities as they quietly departed. In towns and villages where priests proudly took the oath, there were sometimes civic ceremonies, National Guard parades and feasts to mark the occasion. But often, however, wherever authorities, community and priest did not line up unambiguously on the side of revolutionary order, there was conflict.

A mocking depiction from 1790 of clergy and monks
forced to evacuate surplus religious buildings, carrying
off the worldly goods they were not supposed to own.

Some of this had erupted back in November, when news of the oath requirement first broke upon the country. Minor disturbances had been reported in locations from the Pas-de-Calais to Nîmes, while around the lower Loire a wider agitation had flared for several weeks. Municipalities across southern Brittany frequently returned their copies of the decree to higher authorities, refusing to accept its legitimacy. One departmental capital, Vannes, seemed momentarily at risk of siege by columns of protesting peasants. In this region it was quite difficult for a priest actually to take the oath – one Breton clergyman of forty years' seniority lamented to the authorities that he had been stoned by his own parishioners when he attempted it, and in the Vendée, one such cleric was shot.

The rural west was becoming a hotbed of anti-revolutionary resentments, but the oath drew out festering hostilities elsewhere too. In Alsace, oath-takers were abused by crowds, while in the Lozère in the south, knife-wielding female gangs reportedly hounded them from their parishes. Some priests who refused the oath wrote to the authorities explaining that they did so in fear of such consequences – one man from the Haute-Loire, just north of the Lozère, wrote of oath-takers being condemned as 'Judases, traitors and tyrants', part of a plot to change the people's religion.[27]

No corner of the country escaped some reaction. In the high Pyrenean valleys of the Ariège, the market town of Saverdun was riven by claims that 'those who attend the holy services of the constitutional priest will have their tongue pierced, will be branded on their forehead and be shorn'. Along the nearby Boulbonne valley, a short-lived insurrection was based on alarms that 'the constitutional priest's masses are worthless; he breaks his fast and gets drunk before saying them'. In another local village, Suc, the brother of the local non-juring priest tried to lead an uprising to force the authorities to leave him in place.[28]

Such words and deeds reflect a complex collision of material self-interest, genuine (if also self-interested) concern for spiritual efficacy, and a determined belief that religious community was a thing to be safeguarded, if necessary by force. The overall impression created in the minds of the political class, however – proud adherents of enlightened progress, and consumed by belief in patriotic unanimity – was that the rural population was penetrated by a religious 'fanaticism' that posed a real danger to the Revolution. The complementary notion, following on from generations of urban scorn, that the root of this lay in peasant passivity and ignorance, led astray by wily priests, easily took hold.

While in truth much of the rural population remained devoted to the gains they believed they had won in 1789, and continued to prefer a new order to the prospect of reversion to the old, the grating tension between the National Assembly's constitutional vision and the autonomy of the village community continued to grow. It did so as beliefs among other sectors of the common people about the ongoing battle for their freedom against counter-revolution continued to harden.

Urban populations had much to be anxious about in the early months of 1791. There were persistent problems in the supply of basic foodstuffs, as revolutionary administrators tried time and again to wean the French away from their earnest belief that free markets in grain were a licence for exploitative speculations. Unemployment was becoming a scourge in the cities, where much of the population relied on the consumption habits of the elite for their income. Domestic servants and wigmakers were among the most visible economic casualties of an aristocratic elite that was retrenching when it was not actually emigrating. The whole class of artisans, from goldsmiths to saddlers, cabinet makers to glaziers, tailors to ribbon makers, that was at the heart of the urban consumer-goods economy, was experiencing a slump in demand that pinched budgets and heightened anxieties. At every level of society, there was very little grasp of the concept of unintended consequences, and a strong preference to opt for outright blame.

The political tendency to attribute all such distress to deliberate manipulation was aggravated by a very visible, day-by-day fluctuation in the value of *assignat* bonds. Over the previous year these had increasingly come into circulation, contrary to the revolutionaries' original intentions, as a replacement for hard currency that was ever harder to find. As silver and gold coins were hoarded – a predictable piece of economic caution interpreted immediately as a counter-revolutionary plot – and taxes went unpaid, the authorities had had no choice but to fill the gap with paper.

That paper, in its original high-denomination form, in low-value tokens for future interest payments clipped from the original sheets, and in a wide variety of ad hoc substitutes issued by local authorities, had become part of everyday transactions for all social classes by 1791. Alongside these circulated, inevitably, a rising number of outright forgeries, each discovery of which heightened fears of counter-revolutionary destabilization. The unreliability of paper resulted, equally inevitably, in a rise of the value of hard currency against it. Traders refused to take *assignats* without a 10, 15 or even 20 per cent discount against their face value.

A whole ecology of speculative *marchands d'argent*, 'money-sellers', grew up that reached from the Paris stock market to local street corners, luring anxious paper holders with offers of scarce coin. A culture much less paranoid than the one in place under the Revolution would have had no difficulty seeing the rampant dishonesty and exploitation involved in a situation the authorities seemed to have no desire to check.

The expression of that paranoid culture, in which a counter-revolutionary aristocrat lurked behind every piece of news, was becoming more organized, at both local and national levels. The 'Breton Club' of radical National Assembly deputies that had coalesced in the summer of 1789 had formed itself, by the end of that year, into a 'Society of Friends of the Constitution', opened itself to non-deputy subscribers and began to meet regularly in Paris in a former monastic building close to the Tuileries. From the evicted order of monks came its soon-acquired nickname, the Jacobin Club.

Over the course of the next eighteen months, several hundred groups in provincial cities and towns formed in imitation, as respectable professional and properitied men united into a network of ardent and anxious correspondence about the course of the Revolution, and the enemies that threatened it. For such 'Jacobins', there was no contradiction between their networking and the culture of unanimity projected by the constitution's structures: they were not a divisive 'faction', but merely honest patriots united to take a lead on behalf of the nation.

SOCIÉTÉ
DES AMIS
DE LA
CONSTITUTION
Jean ˙ Sevres

To their enemies, of course – and by 1790 this included a majority of all the nobles and clergy within the National Assembly – the Jacobins were precisely a faction, stirring up public agitation, debating the nation's business in a dangerously uncontrolled parallel unofficial structure, and raising demands for new aggressive policies against church and king. This perception intensified in mid-1790, when an even more radical club formed in another ex-monastery, the Cordeliers on Paris's left bank.

A Jacobin club membership card

Like the Jacobins, it held open sessions and attracted an ardent audience of men and women; unlike the Jacobins, it charged a subscription some working people could actually afford.

By the end of 1790, Cordeliers activists had gone a stage further, founding a series of clubs across the city that sought an explicitly mixed-sex membership from the lower classes, and set out to 'educate' such people in the politics of patriotism. The hundreds of people who joined and attended such clubs soon proved to need very little education, and their agenda of hatred of aristocratic conspiracy and anger at official prevarications and compromises soon surpassed what even some Cordeliers members thought fitting. Long months of political tergiversations, in the context of stewing economic strife and uncertainty, and the continuing growth in the number of emigrating aristocrats, had by 1791 brought popular politics in the capital very close to a permanent fever pitch.

The events of 1789 had shown how easy it was to raise angry crowds, and from that summer onwards the public spaces of the city hosted semi-permanent discussions, with hundreds debating the latest news and rumours, and thousands passing through more fleetingly each day. All this debate retained a dangerously violent edge – the line between articulate discussion, angry protest and lynch mobs was wavering, and sometimes erased in an instant, with suspected spies, brigands and conspirators done to death on the streets at several points through 1790. In the spring of 1791, nuns who defied the aftermath of the clerical oath were flogged in public, with press reports gloating over the suffering inflicted on their 'anti-constitutional buttocks'.[29]

The press was the other dimension of the new political culture than had erupted into life. Before the revolutionary crisis, French authors had lived under blanket censorship, that many had circumvented through clandestine publications. Illegal anyway, many of these abandoned any restraint, retailing pornographic rumours about the elite, and generally scurrilous information about the corruption of public life. With censorship thrown off in 1789, such uncompromising attitudes proved irresistibly popular, and those who did attempt to start up a respectable political press found themselves in constant competition, across a broad political spectrum, with those who would print anything that sold.

Several hundred newspapers started up in 1789–91, though most folded after a few weeks or months. There was no linear connection between tone, content and popularity. On the far right of politics, the *Acts of the Apostles* was regularly grossly insulting about the revolutionary leadership, but obscured its abuse (for the uninitiated) in a cloud of allusive language and classical references. For what were thought to be 'uneducated' audiences, pamphleteers of both left and right adopted the blunt and foul-mouthed personae of popular stage characters to get their messages across.

Some journalists strove for higher goals, and the *Feuille villageoise* published over several years an encyclopaedic guide to agricultural improvement and civic engagement – but was mostly read by patriotic clerics and other worthies, rather than the working peasants it hoped to reach. Among the radical agitators of the capital, the most popular authors were men like Jean-Paul Marat, writing in the *Friend of the People*, who never talked down to his readers, but always assailed those in power as hidden counter-revolutionaries, and cried out – under legal assaults from the authorities – for heads to roll to save the people.

Although the frenetic activity of the press formed a distinctive part of the fervid Parisian atmosphere, it also spread across the country by subscription, and Jacobin clubs were particularly avid consumers of the latest alarms, reading them into their minutes and debating their implications, passing resolutions and circulating these to their own regional, and increasingly national,

eh bien, J...F..., dira-tu encore vive la Nobleſſe?

networks. Local news of nefarious aristocratic conduct was almost always available to be folded into the national narrative, and a steady stream of such reports reaching the Paris Jacobins from across the country reaffirmed their own sense of looming threat, and urgent mission.

By the early summer of 1791, that mission, despite all its perils, appeared en route to completion. The National Assembly, in nearly two years of harrowing labours, had remade French public life from scratch, not merely composing a political constitution, but going on to create the outlines of a unified national criminal and civil law code, to recast the notion of military service, of a judiciary and of other facets of life from poor relief to forestry management.

It had done all this under relentless critique from a minority of its own members on the right, and under increasing attack from forces to the left for its unwillingness to boldly confront what they saw as endemic counter-revolutionary subversion. But as the summer solstice approached, decrees had already gone out to prepare for new elections, to round off the completed constitutional monarchy with a new Legislative Assembly, and bring the new machinery of state into its final functioning form. Then, on the morning of 21 June 1791, Paris awoke to discover that the man who was supposed to be the monarchical keystone of the constitution, and his whole family, had fled.

A satirical print offering a potent emblem of a world turned upside-down, as the armed female rider demands profanely of her mount 'Will you still say "Long live the nobility"'?

Treason

Louis XVI and Marie Antoinette had been planning their escape for months. They had played along superficially with their confinement in Paris, but had never stopped regarding themselves as prisoners. The king had intermittently sunk into periods of deep, depressed inactivity, but the queen had maintained an ardently active smuggled correspondence with diplomatic and émigré contacts. As early as February 1791 she had been matter-of-factly sharing in such letters the couple's plans to reconstruct government, reinstate the church, and call the French to renewed loyalty, once beyond the clutches of a city they blamed for all their woes.

Their plans for flight crystallized after a huge crowd had blocked their departure for the chateau of Saint-Cloud in April, where the king had hoped to spend Easter out of the public gaze (and thus, very probably, avoid taking public communion from an oath-taking priest). One of the queen's correspondents, Axel von Fersen, a dashing Swedish knight who may also have been her lover, masterminded the escape. Smuggled out of the city by Fersen himself in a hired coach, the royal couple and their children were loaded into a large six-horse *berline* carriage, which made a rumbling and delayed progress through the countryside eastwards from the city, in the general direction of the frontier fortress of Metz.

Their intention was probably not to leave the country, but to stop in the safe custody of the military garrison and its noble officers, and launch their bid to regain control in the name of the people's true monarchist loyalties. They discovered to their shock that things outside Paris were not as they had fondly believed. Their efforts at disguise were rapidly seen through, and at the small town of Varennes the local officials stopped them, blockading the bridge on the main road to prevent their passage, and summoning townsfolk and peasants alike from a widening circle of alarm to guard against any counter-revolutionary

Caustic satire on the runaway king as a pig: 'I've ruined myself to fatten him up, and I don't know what to do with him any more.'

attempts at recapture. The town council's legal officer, Jean-Baptiste Sauce, a grocer who was himself only barely literate, hosted an extraordinary gathering in his home, during which a former judge fell to his knees upon recognizing the king, and Sauce's elderly mother collapsed sobbing at the thought she was in the presence of royalty.

The king abandoned further pretence, declaring, 'Yes, I am your king, I have come to live among you, my faithful children, whom I will never abandon,' and took the astonishing step of embracing each councilman in turn, before asking for their aid in continuing his journey. Temporarily dazzled, they agreed, before changing their minds and returning to tell the king he could not proceed, that 'he was adored by his people... but that his residence was in Paris... and that the constitution depended on his return'. A local story had it that one man, the old woodcutter Géraudel, was more blunt in the face of royal protestations: 'Sire, we're not sure we can trust you.'[30] As day dawned on 22 June, thousands of

entree franche.

je me suis Ruiné pour l'engresser — la fin du compte je ne sait pu en faire

ARRESTATION DE LOUIS

Louis XVI s'échappa des Thuilleries la nuit du 17 Juin 1791. en menant
frontieres, Le Conducteur de la voiture s'obstina a vouloir changer de chev
menaces, rien ne pût l'engager à marcher, D'autres Chevaux ne se trouvant po
on chercha a savoir quels pouvoit être ces Voyageurs qui témoignoient tant
aux regards du public; Le Maire vin qui reconnu Le Roi, et lui dit qu'il ne p
de la Reine, et de sa famille, rien ne put toucher l'inflexible Maire. Le Roi fu

Frenchmen, armed with everything from regulation muskets to pitchforks, formed a mass that demonstrated clearly that, without any personal hostility to the king, they would not let him pass.

While the people of Varennes had decided spontaneously that the king could not be making his way of his own free will on an innocent country excursion, back in Paris the National Assembly scrambled for a logic that would allow them to control the situation. This was obviously a counter-revolutionary plot, but of whose making? Radicals were already shouting about the marquis de Lafayette's National Guard and its failure to guard the palace. The deputies knew they had to order the detention of the king, or see their constitutional monarchy collapse into rubble, fire and blood.

They declared, from almost the first moments of the flight's discovery, that Louis had been kidnapped, and needed to be rescued. In so doing, they overlooked a declaration in his own hand, left behind in the Tuileries, that abjured all the revolutionary acts he had been forced to acquiesce in, and rejected the whole course of events since June 1789. But the alternative was to declare themselves at war with the king they had always insisted remained the moving spirit and capstone of their efforts.

When word of the king's presence at Varennes reached Paris, the Assembly immediately despatched a party of deputies to accompany his return. Such was the throng of citizens, from town and country alike, that surrounded the coach along the road back to Paris that it progressed at little more than walking pace, giving the royal couple a full taste of the alarm they had provoked, and the patriotic rhetoric of speeches they were forced to listen to at every stop.

That alarm had of course spread nationwide, in a surging wave as news of the flight, the recapture and the progress back to Paris succeeded each other. It touched off something very close to a full-scale invasion panic, with mobilizations little short of martial law in northeastern districts, rumours of 'English' landings from Brittany to Bordeaux, alerts along the Pyrenees and arrests of suspicious non-juring priests scattered from the Nord to the Ariège. Peasants in a number of regions once again turned on seigneurs, with chateau-burnings and at least two murders reported.

Within Paris, the Cordeliers Club took a bold republican stand, and attracted 30,000 signatures on a petition it handed to the Assembly on 24 June. When nearly three weeks later the Assembly finally ruled against any decisive measures, merely 'suspending' the king until he accepted the finished constitution, objections to this split the Jacobin Club. Most deputies left the club, forming a new gathering in yet another ex-monastery, the Feuillants. Remaining more radical Jacobins, and the Cordeliers, tried to organize a new petitioning protest on the Champ de Mars, site of the 1790 Festival of Federation, but a large crowd there was attacked on 17 July by the National Guard, inflamed by rumours of infiltration by counter-revolutionary 'brigands'. The death toll was vigorously disputed, but rumour pushed it into the hundreds. This 'massacre' led to further repression, leaving the agenda of finalizing the constitution in the hands of the centrists.

The upheavals of the summer of 1791 shattered any prospect of the Revolution proceeding relatively peacefully to its goals. The royal couple had negotiated hard with the Feuillant bloc to preserve their position, with their children's safety at stake, and the Feuillant leadership desperately craved royal sanction, against the twin risks of social anarchy and counter-revolutionary assault. Radical leaders had been driven into temporary hiding, and shown in no uncertain terms how much the centrist leadership feared and detested them. New measures in the finalized constitution sought to shut down popular club agitation and petitioning, building on measures passed in the spring that had clamped down on urban workers' agitation, banning strikes and

overleaf
The recaptured royal family, dwindling almost to insignificance in this crude but effective depiction of the massive armed parade that returned them to Paris.

trade unions in the name of the contractual rights of individual citizens.

A hardline consensus in the corridors of power about the radical threat seemed to have solidified. But the Assembly scornfully refused to rise when the king arrived to take his new constitutional oath in September, and in private afterwards, Louis wept at the humiliation, while knowing he had perjured himself, and had no intention of abandoning the priests and nobles suffering degradation at revolutionary hands. Absolutely nothing was safe, secure or settled about this constitutional settlement, even as the Assembly issued a general political amnesty and desperately hoped it could be.

*

The scale of the ongoing conflict between the settlement politicians wanted, and what ordinary people felt they needed, was highlighted again through the summer by rural unrest. On 20 July, a few days after the massacre on the Champ de Mars, there was a major confrontation in the Pays de Caux, near Rouen. An army of up to 4,000 peasants, marching under the banners of no fewer than twenty-two local National Guard units, confronted a military detachment of 200 men sent to guard against disturbances to the harvest. Led by their elected mayors, the peasants issued demands for the withdrawal of the army, and reinstatement of the traditional market controls. The administration of the department responded by sending another 500 men and two cannon to the area, and soliciting a special decree from the Assembly, reaffirming the 'liberty of commerce' in grains.

This incident passed off peacefully, but elsewhere there was a continuing climate of violent confrontation. Harvest labour, done by itinerant gangs in areas of large-scale commercial farming, experienced the same inflationary pressures on wages as townsfolk.

Traditional semi-riotous wage agitation, or *bacchanals*, by such gang members spread widely as a result. The Assembly hastened to extend to rural labourers the ban on economic organization it had imposed on urban workers earlier in the year, and used this new power to send troops against major protest across the Parisian region.

Again and again, the flow of new laws from Paris struck at peasant lives. At a purely practical level, community authorities made up of handfuls of farmers and other local worthies were bludgeoned from Paris with decrees, pronouncements and enactments that arrived at the rate of more than one a day, year in, year out. Simply reading and understanding them, let alone explaining them to constituents, or enacting complex new processes they required, was a burden beyond many. Some gave up and simply returned to the practicalities of life, especially when some of the changes demanded appeared to make no sense.

Rural communities in regions which used 'open field' farming – where crop rotation was organized around large blocks of land, divided into strips owned or rented by individuals – were thrown into perplexity when the Assembly declared that nobody could any longer be forced to follow such a communal practice. In September 1791 new rural and forest law codes came into force, reiterating the individualist rights of property owners. On the one hand, owners of livestock could no longer be compelled to keep them in a communal herd, and owners of land no longer had to give right of way to such herds. On the other, claims of customary access for poorer individuals to gather firewood or other resources from communal woodlands were erased.

Part of the ongoing rural tension since 1789 had been the invasion by peasants of uncultivated 'wastes' and woods kept out of their hands by seigneurial rules. Local administrators often bewailed this as an assault on the landscape, and a real ecological danger. There was evidence that clearing of hillsides, for example, could provoke flash floods; and in general, stripping woodlands without careful consideration always risked depleting a resource which could take decades to regenerate. But here as in so many other aspects of life, the National Assembly simply imposed blanket bans and expected them to be enforced, regardless of local sentiments or needs.

The constitutionally decreed Legislative Assembly took up its duties in October 1791, a completely new body of men after its predecessor had barred its own members from standing, eager to be done with the burdens and conflicts of the past two years. Although there were now no counter-revolutionaries in the actual legislature, many of the new deputies were adept at spotting them at every other level of power, and particularly in the circles around the reinstated king. Louis XVI soon found himself confronted with radical Jacobin-inspired legislation demanding harsh penalties against non-juring clergy and émigré aristocrats, and surprised nobody by exercising his new constitutional veto power. Behind the scenes, centrist Feuillant advisors despaired at failure to develop a constructive politics, and in public, a drumbeat of patriotic demands for a war against the émigrés and their foreign supporters grew louder.

The Legislative Assembly's essential problem was that literally none of the cans of worms opened since 1789 had been successfully closed. August 1791, indeed, saw an epochal new one opened, as the 500,000 slaves of France's flagship Caribbean colony, Saint-Domingue, took advantage of deadly political strife among the local white and 'free coloured' populations to launch their own violent bid for freedom. The effects of this took some time to filter through to the metropolitan nation, but in the meantime, it had troubles enough.

The northwestern quadrant of France remained profoundly disrupted and alienated from the revolutionary settlement. Its departments had sent a solid contingent of radical deputies to the new Assembly, because almost nobody outside the circles of middle-class urban club members bothered to vote. An official investigation of ongoing unrest in the region found that town-based administrations felt effectively under siege from 'fanatical' peasants in thrall to non-juring clergy, who thronged the area despite being officially deposed. From the peasant perspective, local power had fallen into the hands of a class they knew only as rapacious absentee landlords, unlike their familiar village priests or local gentry in every way, and the revolutionary authorities kept reinforcing their alienation, both economically and culturally.

The leadership of the Maine-et-Loire department wrote to the Assembly in November 1791, documenting their own fears at reports that 'assemblies of three or four thousand armed men form at several points', animated by 'the delirious excesses of superstition and fanaticism'. Three of their subsidiary district capitals were, they claimed, in imminent 'danger of night attacks, of being pillaged and burnt by these brigands'. The writers pledged to 'die here rather than abandon' their posts, and pointedly added that the 'interest of religion' that the peasants claimed could only be a transparent cover for real counter-revolutionary intent.[31]

With varying degrees of intensity, all these problems could be found elsewhere as well: through the previous summer a quarter of all departmental administrations had petitioned for a law exiling non-juror priests, or had gone further and taken their own, strictly illegal, action against them. Around Lyon, local officials reported a state of 'latent insurrection' in the countryside; around Toulouse, administrators declared that religious liberty had to be limited to 'the honest citizen', prepared to exercise it with 'respect for public order'.[32] What this meant in practice appeared in departments from the far north to Brittany and the southeastern Ardèche: armed National Guard sweeps through the countryside, seizing non-jurors, and sometimes their supporters, and their property. The village of Berlaimont in the Nord, singled out as a haunt of resistance, was assailed by men from fifteen neighbouring communities, who pillaged the local convent.

As the campaign for war among Jacobins and patriots gathered strength through the winter, so too did the hostility to priests and their supporters: by the spring of 1792 almost half of all departments had taken direct action against them. Some Jacobin groups, such as those of Angers, Besançon and Montauban, attempted a more positive agenda. They created 'ambulatory clubs' to conduct what was essentially political missionary activity in their rural hinterlands. Unfortunately the unyielding anti-clerical dogmatism and blinkered general approach to rural grievances they took into this work created a strong correlation between their movements and later persistent counter-revolutionary sympathies.

Another side to popular antagonism to the authorities was their complete failure to act effectively for the relief of poverty. The country at large had never really recovered from the crisis of 1788–9, which had plunged a fifth of the population into destitution. Industries of all kinds struggled to profit in a time of radical uncertainty, and unemployment was a scourge. Each time the elite responded with measures such as subsidized labouring work in 'public workshops', the demand for places was such that the workers became a terrifying threat and burden, and the workshops were forcibly disbanded: this happened in Paris in 1789, and again in the agitated summer of 1791. Across the country, some public works projects, notably canal building, did endure more successfully, but could only give work to thousands, in a situation where millions feared poverty.

Attacking the parochial organization of the church, and its independent income, had crippled the longstanding networks of basic charitable relief, and bold plans to create a state-funded network of civic institutions of *bienfaisance* – 'doing good' in place of 'sterile' charity – came to nothing in the absence of stable tax receipts. Religiously founded hospitals were exempted from the sale of their property as *biens nationaux*, but were obliged to pay new taxes on that property, and in 1792 lost the right to claim income from it. State funds promised in recompense almost never arrived, and thus time-honoured structures of care for widows and orphans, the old, the sick and crippled fell into almost complete dilapidation.

The social divide between popular and Jacobin expectations was shown in the first months of 1792, as the revolt in Saint-Domingue fed through into shortages and steep price rises for sugar and coffee. These previously relatively cheap stimulants had become staples of the urban working-class diet, and serious unrest followed, including price-fixing attacks on Parisian grocers' shops. The political class was shocked at such concern for what they chose to regard as luxuries, and many Jacobin clubs proclaimed that they would abstain from sugar and coffee as a 'patriotic' act of self-denial – implicitly, and sometimes explicitly, criticizing those in the lower orders unwilling to do the same.

Focusing attention on the riots in Paris meant that Jacobins need not display so much concern for yet another crisis in basic provisioning, erupting through the winter of 1791–2 after poor weather had waterlogged autumn fields and caused flooding across much of southeastern France. Grain prices shot up by between a quarter and a half, with *assignat* inflation effectively doubling the increase for those without hard cash. In the countryside around Paris, in the market towns and river ports of the Aisne and the Oise valleys, as well as further north and east, whole communities turned out to demand 'just prices' by force, often with their mayors and National Guard emblems on parade.

Thousands of peasants marched on the towns, bringing with them rural workers like pin makers, weavers and charcoal burners to mingle with the poorer classes of the urban labour force, and sometimes with local lawyers, forge masters or land stewards lending their presence. There were even some constitutional priests who took the opportunity to preach apocalyptic sermons against the evils of the property owners. All of this, to the national authorities, was simply unacceptable disorder. When in March 1792 the mayor of Étampes, a major grain-trade centre in the Seine-et-Oise, was killed in a confrontation with a price-fixing crowd, the response of the Legislative Assembly was to make him a martyr for the cause of revolutionary legality, later holding a 'Festival of the Law' in his honour.

While the country could be violently divided by such issues, the common people could also erupt into direct action to protect the Revolution. Early in 1792, in the southwestern Lot department, chateaux belonging to seigneurs suspected of joining the enemy ranks were attacked; nearby in the Tarn, non-jurors and suspicious aristocrats were assaulted, and the latter sometimes formally 'disarmed' by National Guards. Around the regional capital Toulouse, thousand-strong peasant bands were reported to be engaged in a complex agenda of actions from price-fixing protests to harassment of non-jurors and the burning of feudal titles. Similar actions convulsed several departments of central France.

Meanwhile, in the southeast, sectarianism and virulent anti-clericalism occasioned endemic low-level violence and occasional flares of more decisive action. On 20 February 1792 a second gathering of Catholic loyalists at Jalès dispersed before a retaliatory expedition of Protestant forces could reach them – but the latter clashed with locals, leaving seven dead, and a Catholic leader turned up drowned in the Rhône a few days later. In the flashpoint town of Nîmes, price-fixing riots in March led to further violence that was fanned by both royalist and patriot reactions, with waves of rural chateau attacks, price fixing and assaults on anyone associated with either administration or continuing contests over feudal rights. Sectarian, royalist/patriot, urban/rural, and rich/poor divides were blending into a state of permanent paranoid anxiety and readiness for violent responses to any perceived threat.

Amid all this, it was tragically inevitable that the whole political class would lunge towards external war as a solution. Jacobins understood all disorder as the product of émigré counter-revolutionary subversion, that only victory could repel. Centrists and Feuillants, including figures such as Lafayette, saw an injection of wartime discipline as the answer to their perception of destabilizing Jacobin excess. The king, the queen and their inner circle thought – ludicrously, and suicidally – that a swift defeat for the Revolution would bring the country crawling back to them.

So it was that on 20 April 1792 France declared war on the 'king of Hungary and Bohemia', many-titled Habsburg ruler of Austria, after months of mutually provocative demands about the treatment of nobles and émigrés, and with firm expectations of victory on all sides. War, the organization of war and the further internal ruptures it was to generate, would raise up the forces of popular patriotism to almost unimaginable heights of commitment. But it would also see a horrifying component of that force turned on those among the French themselves who could not accept the definition of patriotic conduct the Revolution demanded. The years to come would doom all those who took the lead in advocating war, and claim a still-greater toll of lives from the common people.

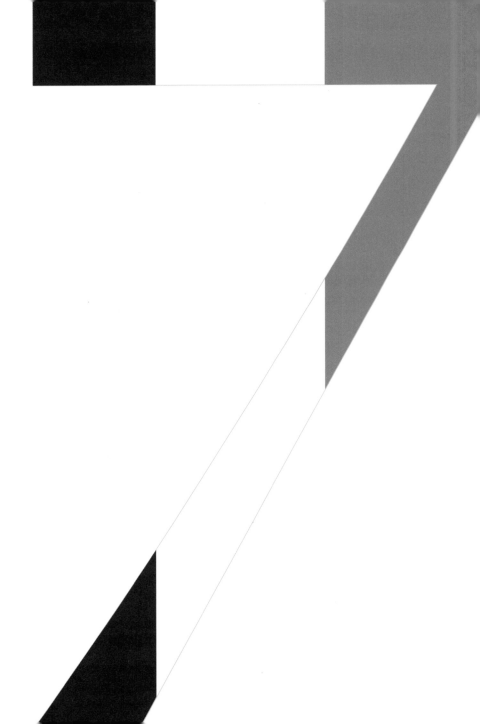

War, Massacre and Terror

The war was supposed to be a rout of the decadent aristocratic enemy and the unwilling 'slaves of despotism' they conscripted into their armies. The leading group of pro-war Jacobins around the journalist and politician Jacques-Pierre Brissot had promised as much. The French army, destabilized by the trauma of 1789 and by the emigration of many noble officers, had suffered debilitating mutinies in 1790, but soldiers had been offered new citizenship rights from 1791, which politicians believed had bolstered its revolutionary enthusiasm. Numbers under arms had been boosted by an influx of 100,000 men to new volunteer units after the royal escape attempt. Such units, with different uniforms and higher pay rates than the regulars, had been enrolled for one year only.

An army divided among itself, and uncertain of its commanders' loyalties (almost every senior officer still in post was a noble), was ordered on to the offensive in the Austrian Netherlands, and effectively disintegrated upon meeting resistance. Officers, including one general, were lynched by panicking troops crying out against betrayal. Only the slow-moving nature of the enemy advances saved France from entirely catastrophic military collapse, and when Prussia joined the war in the summer (and one-year volunteers started to walk away from the front lines), such a threat loomed terrifyingly large.

By that stage, in early July 1792, the constitutional monarchy had essentially collapsed. The political class reacted with a confused mix of shock and decisiveness to military reverses. 'Patriot' ministers linked to Brissot's circle shuffled in and out of government, in increasingly open conflict with the king himself. On 20 June a massive popular demonstration burst into the Tuileries and physically confronted Louis with demands for action, but could do nothing more than shout at him. A week later, the marquis de Lafayette, who had failed to be elected mayor of Paris and taken up a commanding general's post on the front lines, left his army and came to the capital in a short-lived bid to launch a military coup against Jacobin radicalism. Left and right united to scorn him, and he withdrew back to his command, astonishingly surviving an attempt at impeachment – such were the divisions and confusions of the moment.

On 5 July, the Legislative Assembly created a series of emergency measures of civil and military mobilization, under the heading of 'The Fatherland in Danger'. Attempts over the previous month to get the king to act in a similar fashion had come to nothing, and on 11 July the Assembly enacted this decree on its own authority. The National Guard was militarized for external service, all administrative bodies were called into permanent daily session, and the royal veto was rendered effectively null and void. Although the king was still theoretically the head of the executive branch, the Assembly had already deposed him in practice.

Over the following month, radical belief in Paris that, despite his sidelining, the king was still the centre of counter-revolutionary threat intensified. A 'Manifesto' written by an émigré and issued in the name of the duke of Brunswick, the allied commander advancing from the east, reached the capital at the start of August. It threatened to raze the city to the ground if Louis XVI were harmed or insulted. Neighbourhood 'section' assemblies, meeting under the Fatherland in Danger provisions, began to petition for his overthrow, but the Legislative Assembly could not agree to act.

Parisian radicals in the clubs, sections and National Guard high command took the initiative, and on 10 August a massive armed advance on the Tuileries prompted the king to surrender into the custody of the Assembly for his family's safety. In fleeing, Louis failed to order his Swiss Guards to stand down, and their defiance of Parisian demands to surrender led to an outbreak of firing, followed by an overwhelming massacre of several hundred

LE SERMENT RÉPUBLICAIN.

qu'on apprit à Paris que les Autrichiens, et Prussiens étoient dans les plaines de Châlons ;
Citoyens firent le serment, et le signèrent de leur sang, de ne point rentrer chez eux qu'ils n'eussent
ribués à chasser les ennemis hors de la france.

Des Citoyens chantants l'hyme des Marseillois,... ils en sont au refr...
aux armes Citoyens!..........

troops, and the enraged looting and burning of the palace's fitments. With several hundred patriot wounded and dead as well, this essentially accidental bloodbath set a grim tone for what was to follow.

The fall of the monarchy was a largely Parisian affair, although aided by several thousand of the most radical National Guard activists, brought to the capital by the Fatherland in Danger measures. The contingent from Marseille, passing through military encampments on their way north, had picked up the newly written 'Battle Hymn of the Rhine Army', and their renderings gave it a new name, the *Marseillaise*. Such national unifying messages were not the only ones on display in the wider country, however.

In the northwest, local authorities continued hunting down non-juror priests, inflaming rural sentiments ever further with every armed raid. When a national call for 50,000 new 'volunteers' for military service went out in late July, and local quotas were decreed for the recruitment, there was profound unrest. On 21 August, a force of over 10,000 peasants invaded the capital of the Deux-Sèvres department and destroyed its administrative records. They were heard to claim that foreign powers were acting

to defend the true religion. Across Brittany, National Guards who had been called into service for the war found themselves instead defending local centres under threat of peasant siege. In the Mayenne, protestors declared unequivocally that they would 'never consent to send soldiers against the king and the priests'.[33]

Elsewhere, the flow of sentiments went in the reverse direction, and popular violence against counter-revolutionaries sometimes passed beyond official control. In the Ardèche and the Gard, crowds murdered aristocratic and clerical suspects in several centres in mid-July, simultaneous with a furious National Guard attack on a third gathering of Catholic forces at Jalès. Two priests were lynched in Bordeaux, previously relatively unscathed by violence, and in August at Port-en-Bessin in Normandy the authorities had to save a large party of priests from local wrath, as their gathering to emigrate prompted fears of an invasion attempt.

Toppling the monarchy only redoubled such fears, since now the proclaimed revenge of the émigrés was sure to be enacted. The provisional authorities closed down the overtly royalist press, which had continued preaching hatred of Jacobin subversion until its last hours. As Lafayette confirmed his treacherous status by asking his army to march on Paris, and fleeing to the enemy when it refused, the Austro-Prussian army pressed on, reaching Verdun on 29 August. Brushing aside a token force outside its walls, and taking the fortifications after a brief four-day siege, they saw the road to Paris open before them.

This threat, apparent since late August, produced another surge in patriotic rhetoric and mobilization in Paris, and preparations for forces to leave the city for a last-ditch defence. With hundreds of counter-revolutionary suspects recently rounded up and stuffed into an already ramshackle prison system, beset with rumours of corruption and subversion, the final stage of those preparations was massacre.

Massacre at the Tuileries palace on 10 August 1792, one of a series of remarkable eye-witness images produced by the artist Etienne Bericourt, previously known only for watercolours of popular fairs and amusements.

Maxime Faivre

The 'September Massacres' lasted from the 2nd to the 5th, and claimed around 1,500 lives. Most of those killed were common criminals, understood by the population at large to be corruptible 'brigands' likely to take aristocratic pay. Among the detained clergy and aristocrats, the radical activists who invested the prisons took care to make evidence-based judgments. Impromptu 'tribunals' read arrest records and conducted interrogations, and decided to save at least as many as they condemned. Those they doomed were usually hacked to death unceremoniously in nearby courtyards. None of them were guilty of the tentacular plot their killers chose to believe in, but most had given contradictory or defiant answers. In scale these events were appalling, and spawned spiralling legends of cannibalistic popular fury, but they were ironically the outcome of a more discriminating process than many individual political killings that had marked the preceding years.

Across France, the same sense of crisis that drove the Parisian massacres produced more waves of lynching. Four men died in Marseille, and a larger number were detained to await the judgments of a new 'popular tribunal'. Crowds in Lyon stormed the prisons, dragging out three priests and eight military officers to their deaths. A group of fifty counter-revolutionary suspects, due to be tried in Orléans, but transferred to Saumur, were intercepted en route in Versailles, and done to death.

Frequently, the rallying of volunteers for service and preemptive judgment of counter-revolutionaries ran hand in hand. Across the Orne department of Normandy, six different sites saw the killing of a total of nine men by such groups between mid-August and early September. In Reims, midway between Paris and besieged Verdun, news of the latter's fall sparked two days of uprising that killed a local official, six priests and a noble. Over sixty such deadly incidents took place across the country. In at least fifteen departments, such mobilization also accompanied

previous pages
An extraordinarily vivid image of the common people of Paris in 1792, imagined by the artist Léon-Maxime Faivre in 1908, gazing at the exposed corpse of the Princesse de Lamballe: an event which itself probably never happened.

violence against elite property and the persistent survival of the feudal burden. In one particularly telling case in the Jura, mobilized National Guards from rural communities seized and destroyed the records of the state office charged with collecting feudal payments owed on nationalized church lands – a reminder that the revolutionary state continued to monetize every aspect of these assets, at the peasantry's expense.

Even while such incidents highlighted certain kinds of popular zeal, and while overall the 'Second Revolution' of the fall of the monarchy led to a thorough-going purge of administrative ranks, genuine fervour was not as widely spread as radicals might have hoped. The volunteers who had come forward in 1791 had been something approaching a cross-section of the active male population, including many men in their twenties and thirties. Filling quotas in the summer of 1792, even outside the regions of active resistance, was harder.

Many local authorities had to pay cash bounties, which by definition only incentivized the poor and desperate. Some communities undertook ballots, in a process alarmingly close to ostracism, while others nudged youths with quarrels and misdemeanours hanging over them into enlistment. Three-quarters of all the 1792 volunteers were under twenty-five, and most were poor peasants. As with the 1791 cohort, they understood their enlistment to be for one year at most, and many would take that to mean one campaign season.

Fortunately for France, the campaign that mixed forces of regulars and volunteers opened by confronting the advancing allied army at Valmy, on the same road the king had fled down the previous year, was glorious. A brief engagement on 20 September was enough to persuade the enemy leadership to shorten their supply lines and withdraw into winter quarters on friendly territory. With pressure eased in the east, reinforcement to the north led to a historic victory against inferior Austrian forces at

Jemappes in early November, and by the middle of that month French forces had occupied Brussels, and were on their way to complete control of the Austrian Netherlands.

A new National Convention, elected (by the patriot and activist circles still taking part in elections) to decide the constitutional future of the nation, had declared France a Republic, 'one and indivisible', almost simultaneously with the Valmy victory, and promised a new vision of democratic and popular government. But achieving that vision for a nation still largely made up of peasants continued to perplex the elite of lawyers, schoolmasters, ex-clerics and other property owners who formed the Convention.

*

At the end of its life, the Legislative Assembly had struck down all feudal rights for which owners could not produce 'original titles', after endless petitioning and persistent direct action by peasant communities. But it also reaffirmed that rents could be increased by the value of abolished dues, and insisted on the legal enforcement of all dues for which such titles did exist – notably those now gathered by the state on church lands, and on an increasing quantity of confiscated émigré property as well.

Through the winter of 1792–3, the Convention attempted yet again to enforce a deregulation of the grain trade, in defiance of still further waves of price-fixing riots around the country. Meanwhile it cancelled another measure of the Legislative Assembly that would have allowed for the division of common lands within communities, scorning a significant petition campaign in its favour. A growing wave of rural anger about the denial of this possibility was met in March 1793 with a decree ordaining the death penalty for anyone proposing the forcible redistribution of land – which was not what most advocates of commons division wanted, but which, labelled with the ancient Roman tag of the *lex agraria*, symbolized how little the Convention cared about what they did want.

The constitutional monarchy had made the totem of its sovereign power 'the nation', running that term alongside 'the law' through the Declaration of Rights, and joining both with 'the king' in the oaths it regularly demanded of officials and citizens. The new Republic would make 'citizen' into a form of address, for both men and women – though it would never seriously contemplate giving female *citoyennes* political rights, and banned them from public gatherings in late 1793. It raised up 'the people' to shibboleth status alongside 'the nation', while imposing ever-stricter definitions on what actual people were allowed to do, say or think, and remain members of that body.

It was aided in doing this by a new term, invented almost out of whole cloth (and probably out of an obscure literary joke) to describe those who eagerly put themselves forward as patriotic friends of the people in early 1792. *Sans-culottes*, 'without knee-breeches', first surfaced as a right-wing dig at men like Brissot and his pro-war patriots, but by the summer of that year had jumped to being a defiant self-applied label for the activists in the Parisian sections, and those like the Marseillais who had joined in the overthrow of the monarchy. Reinterpreted along the way to embrace a (largely false) notion that real working men wore long trousers, *sans-culottes* by 1793 had become both a political movement in itself, and an ideal all were supposed to aspire to.

At the core of *sans-culottes* identity was the paradox of a gruff, foul-mouthed masculinity of honest working men, paraded as a virtue by journalists such as Jacques-René Hébert, who had never done a day's manual work in his life, and taken up by the leadership of the Parisian sections, more of whom were clerks and teachers than actual wage earners. A majority of the sections' activists and committee members might once have been workers, but had become employers of labour as master artisans and shopkeepers – and many of these had taken up the allowances and opportunities of local office holding to replace income lost in the collapse of the luxury trades. Some among the most notable activists played up the *sans-culottes* image particularly hard, because they were in fact well-established property owners, and even gentry, who had thrown in their lot with radical anti-aristocratic politics.

Sansculotterie was as much a political movement, and a faction in republican politics, as it was any kind of social identity, but it was projected as a mode of being for the whole common people – utterly devoted to the Republic, paranoidly suspicious of its enemies, self-sacrificing in militant action, unquestioningly adherent to prevailing orthodoxy – that represented a brutal trap for anyone who could not combine all those qualities. As the politics of the new Republic played out through 1793 and 1794, and what history calls 'the Terror', many of the common people, in city and country, would fall into that fatal snare.

*

The Terror was, fundamentally, two processes: a mobilization for war against counter-revolution on an unprecedented, socially transformative scale, and a spiral of mutual suspicion and hatred within the revolutionary political class about who was betraying whom to the nation's enemies. Both processes overlapped and intertwined, as they had done since before the fall of the monarchy, and in both of them the common people were summoned to obedient action, and suffered grievously for any attempt to resist. The power of the propaganda unleashed on them, and the real gain that a majority still saw from the promises of 1789, stirred enormous forces into action, but directed many of them into what was increasingly overt civil war.

The politics of the Republic's elite were cursed at their birth by a collision between the formerly radical grouping around

Brissot and factions further to their left. Brissot's associates had manoeuvred their way into royal ministerial office in 1792, desperately trying to make the war effort work, and tried to resist calls to overthrow the monarchy, fearing chaos and defeat. This made them compromised traitors in the eyes of those who launched the 10 August assault, and the Brissotins reciprocated the feeling by accusing ultra-radical leaders – the municipal politician Georges-Jacques Danton, journalist Marat and radical hero of the National Assembly Maximilien Robespierre – of trying to have them rounded up and despatched in the September Massacres. Yet neither side's grip on power was secure enough to do down the other.

When all these leading figures found seats in the National Convention, and began to debate the fate of the king, their festering hatreds merely grew. Brissotins now became nicknamed Girondins, as several of their leading speakers came from Bordeaux, in the Gironde department, and were often disparaged for representing selfish mercantile interests. The ultra-radicals secured a position dominating the left side of acceptable discourse, and were labelled Montagnards, the mountain men who sat in the highest-tiered benches of the Convention, and also represented the purity that contemporary literature associated with Alpine virility and independence. *Sans-culottes* activists favoured the Montagnards, not without reservations, but were violently antagonistic to the Girondins.

By January 1793 the Convention had agreed that Louis XVI, dubbed 'Citizen Capet' when stripped of his titles, was a guilty traitor, but it split down the middle on what to do with him. Montagnards were for death, Girondins for a variety of temporizing alternatives, including the possibility of a referendum on his sentence. Each accused the other of nefarious motives: Girondins were simply trying to save him, while Montagnards wanted to inflame their enemies' commitment against the nation.

He was sent for execution by a sixty-vote majority, with several hundred Girondins and other moderates thus identified for future radical attention.

Stormy and sometimes physical disputes rocked the floor of the Convention, and by the early spring Girondins launched a series of political attacks on *sans-culottes* leaders they accused of threatening a chaotic overthrow of the national representation – reviving charges of aspiring dictatorship they had flung at Robespierre six months earlier. A dramatic and entirely political acquittal of the journalist Marat, who had very much called for his enemies' heads, turned the tables, and by the end of May *sans-culottes* forces were rallying to impose a purge of the Girondin leadership on the Convention. Montagnard leaders acquiesced in this, though hesitant about intruding extra-legal force so close to the heart of the Republic, and over two dozen Girondins were ousted by a Convention surrounded by tens of thousands of mobilized Parisians on 2 June 1793.

This had shattering consequences for the country at large, and accelerated the process of narrowing ideological purity at the centre. Girondin-supporting newspapers had already been attacked by *sans-culottes* crowds, and now melted away. Executive power was concentrated in a Committee of Public Safety within the Convention, joined by Robespierre in late July, and a new constitution drafted in the summer was suspended in the autumn until 'revolutionary government' had saved the Republic from war.

Amid new waves of mobilizing legislation, tensions in the anti-Girondin coalition soon broke out into violent and threatening language. By the late autumn of 1793, groups around Danton had begun to be labelled as compromisers, seeking peace at the cost of displaying a disturbing openness to negotiation with counter-revolutionaries. On the other hand, *sans-culottes* leaders around the journalist Hébert and the Cordeliers Club were making dangerous claims about the corruption of the Convention's leadership, and a need for more purges.

Robespierre in particular was ever alert to hints of corruption, and by the late winter had far more than hints in hand, as several figures fearful of being compromised handed over suggestive evidence, and made much more far-reaching accusations of conspiracy. A new wave of deadly purges in the spring, beginning with the suspiciously foreign contacts of Hébert and his supposedly plebeian *sans-culottes* allies, widened to take in Danton and other former friends of Robespierre, that his purity forced him to abandon.

Over the next months, down to July 1794, men who had a year or two earlier been the closest of ideological allies found new reasons to turn on each other with accusations of treason, and of having always hidden counter-revolution in their hearts. The political class began to tear itself apart, until some of the survivors – men of blood among them – saved their own lives by denouncing Robespierre in the same terms he had denounced others: as a secret counter-revolutionary and aspiring tyrant. 'The Terror' thus ended on 27 July 1794 (9 Thermidor in the new 'Republican Calendar'), by consuming itself.

While all this had been taking place, the Convention had mobilized the nation for a war which had increasingly also become a civil war. The collision between the paranoid politics of the centre, and the real carnage across the landscape of France, has helped create the epic terms in which these events are often discussed. But in many respects they were a continuing escalation of the conflicts that had been underway for years, and in which the peasantry of France were as much victims as participants.

The Republic
and the People

The months of February and March 1793, in which the first legislative landmarks of the Terror were laid down, saw renewed collisions between the common people and the revolutionary elite, and more evidence of the basic divides that would give the following eighteen months their awful character. Raging price inflation, particularly for sugar and soap, saw another wave of price-fixing riots in Paris, and intensified scorn from radical leaders. Robespierre spoke of rioters as 'a mob of women, led by valets of the aristocracy', while another leading spokesman denounced 'the perfidious incitement of aristocrats in disguise', and warned that 'where I see no respect for property, there I can no longer recognize any social order'.[34]

At almost the same moment as these riots, the Convention demanded a massive new effort of military mobilization, seeking a levy of 300,000 men – volunteers if possible, but with compulsion by lot or ballot as a back-up. This was particularly critical as the Convention now expanded the war with declarations against Spain, the Dutch Republic, Britain and the Italian states, convinced that all were already part of an aristocratic conspiracy to destroy the Republic. Within two weeks, the response to this had become so alarming that the Convention began to send out teams of its own members, dubbed Representatives-on-Mission, with plenipotentiary authority to manage local politics. The situation they faced, even at this early stage, was little less than catastrophic.

Most of the northern and eastern border regions, under direct threat of invasion, raised their recruits successfully, although rarely could they rely entirely on volunteers to do so. When some 1791 volunteers agreed to return to the colours, it was notable enough to merit local celebrations, as occurred in the Haute-Saône and Doubs departments. Demographers have identified 1793 as the year of a sharp spike in marriages, as the unmarried men in their twenties and thirties targeted by the levy took one obvious course of action to avoid it.

Such bachelor groups frequently also objected to the specific exemption given to those who held public office or served in the National Guard. Where such strata already appeared as oppressors of the peasantry, reactions could be deeply hostile. In town after town, angry crowds gathered demanding that officials, local Jacobins and purchasers of *biens nationaux* show their patriotism by signing up first. In Semur-en-Auxois a ballot exercise proposed the sons of the local wealthy elite for service; elsewhere, constitutional priests found their names put forward on similar lists.

Discontent and dissent reached even the most remote areas. Gaspard Rousse, a peasant farmer from the hamlet of Arconac, high in the Pyrenean valleys of the Ariège, was denounced for saying that 'the nation has begun to lay its hands on our persons'. To another man's patriotic demand that 'we must all rush to help the nation', Rousse retorted that 'since he was speaking that way, they should send *him*'. Two Dordogne sharecroppers, Barrot and Chaveroche, told volunteers that France's enemies 'were angry at the *Bourgeois*, not at the peasants' and, echoing the widespread view elsewhere, that they should go to the district 'to make the office holders march off to war'.[35]

Representatives-on-Mission, finding such unpalatable events, widely insisted on instituting lotteries, but the result, particularly in more isolated and upland areas, was young men taking to the hills with their families' collusion, beginning a tradition of draft-evading *insoumission* that would endure for years to come. Locally, things could get much worse. In the Aveyron department, potential conscripts rioted on 17 March, injuring the mayor of Rodez, and several thousand men rose in a brief insurgency that required direct military intervention, and the execution of twenty ringleaders, as it crossed over into overt counter-revolutionary incitement. This was only a skirmish, however, compared to events in the northwest of France.

overleaf
Anti-revolutionary guerrilla fighters, dramatically depicted by the nineteenth century Breton artist Léonce Petit.

A nineteenth-century engraving, imagining
the dramatic beginnings of the Vendéen rebellion.

A dozen departments across western Normandy, Brittany and the lower Loire valley – closely correlated with majority refusal of the 1791 clerical oath – were pushed into varying degrees of insurrection by the February levy. In Brittany, district capitals, and even the major city of Rennes, were briefly threatened with being overrun by columns of aggrieved peasants. A huge National Guard mobilization was needed to break the threat, along with fifty public executions. Although the levy was successfully imposed in April, those it left behind now coalesced into a guerrilla movement dubbed the *Chouans*, destroying signs and symbols of republicanism in their communities, and leaving the town-based authorities functioning as if military occupiers, subject to random ambush if they left their armed camps.

South of here, in the region soon identified by the name of one department at its heart, the Vendée, a similar but far more thorough-going insurrection shattered the fragile web of republican authority. Conscription was the final spark to a fire of rebellion that had been stoked by every prejudiced and short-sighted attack that urban revolutionaries had launched on these communities' culture. Peasant crowds invaded local capitals, destroying records and declaring themselves for church and king.

By the first half of March, combat had already produced hundreds of casualties, as National Guards tried and failed to move in on the rebels. The ebb and flow of victories and defeats, advances and retreats, produced threatening concentrations of prisoners on both sides, and a grim cycle of massacre and retaliation took hold. By the end of March, numerous incidents of the execution of dozens of republicans, and several running into the hundreds, had cemented a fight to the death.

The Convention drove this home on 19 March by voting the death penalty without appeal for rebels. Renewed justification for such desperate measures appeared days later, when news arrived that French armies pushing north into the Dutch Republic had been disastrously defeated at Neerwinden, and were streaming southwards in a rout that quickly reversed all the gains of the previous campaign. When the defeated General Dumouriez, a close ally of the Girondin leadership, echoed Lafayette by denouncing radicals in Paris, trying to lead his army in a coup, then fled on 5 April to Austrian lines, the reverberations between the politics of the centre and the country only grew sharper.

The Convention also created in March 1793 a Revolutionary Tribunal, to judge all acts of political treachery without appeal. In the face of growing *sans-culottes* demands for action, the radical orator Danton had memorably framed this decision as a means of retaining control over the kind of forces that had been unleashed in the September Massacres: 'Let us be terrible, so as to save the people from being so!'[36] While this played into the convenient legend of popular violence as an anonymous, unstoppable force to be placated, the actual *sans-culottes* activists of Paris were engaged in a very visible process of taking over those local sections that did not agree with them. 'Fraternization' involved marching in large numbers to local meetings, demanding the replacement of the neighbourhood leaders with more suitable candidates, and imposing the result by 'acclamation', with the threat of a beating for anyone who dissented.

After this process had been completed, and accompanied by the appointment of new delegates to the central Parisian mu-nicipality, the Commune, activists turned to summoning up a massive rank-and-file, paid with official funds, to march under arms and demand the deposition of the Girondins at the end of May. At the very same time they were doing this, similar ordinary working people were being rallied in their thousands in Lyon and Marseille to resist the chaotic interference of intruding Jacobin representatives. Such agents, whipped up by the Parisian conflict, had begun to see the whole populations of these cities as corrupt-ed by Girondin mercantile tendencies.

overleaf
Lesueur depictions of a variety of urban tradesmen
armed for volunteer service. (Musée Carnavalet).

Sans-Culotte avec sa redoutable pique.

Chartier faisant sa faction

fort de la halle

r sa garde.

Savetier allant monter
sa garde

Menuisier en faction
revetu de sa houpelande

Volontaire partant pour l'Armée
avec un uniforme qui n'a pas
été imité

Lors de la guerre de la V
qui étoit cacochiome, et
prendre soin de son fils qu

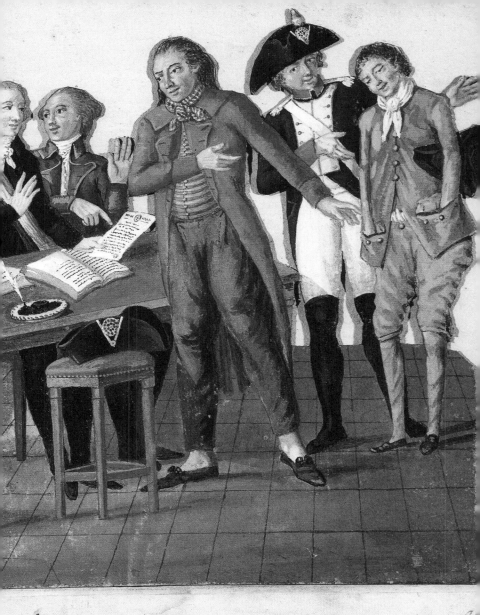

on fit des Réquisitions de jeunes gens. un Citoyen présenta son fil.
imbécile, et incapable de servir; Mais il proposa que si l'on vo
cheroit à sa place; ce qui fut accepté.

Even before the Parisian purge began, 25,000 Marseillais had petitioned the Convention to recall and punish representatives whose choice of ultra-radical local allies was destabilizing the entire region. On 29 May, just in time for news to reach Paris and colour the final purge on 2 June, Lyon rose in revolt against its own local government, after news that the latter had called for troops to march on the city. These revolts coupled with unrest in Bordeaux and Normandy after the Girondins' ousting to produce a movement denounced as a 'Federalist' threat to the one and indivisible Republic. They were the flashpoints of a much wider landscape of social and political chaos.

Both the dominant Montagnards and their new Federalist enemies attempted to impose a simplifying social reading of the breakdown in progress. For the latter, radical Jacobins had proved themselves to be fatal advocates of 'anarchy', who had spent the past year inflaming their gullible plebeian supporters against republican statesmen, with the nefarious objective of enriching themselves from the plunder of the public sphere. For such radicals themselves, the Girondins and their provincial supporters were false friends of the people, advocating passivity where mobilization was needed, and essentially driven by the selfish greed of a mercantile oligarchy seeking to secure its dominance. The aristocratic counter-revolution and its foreign allies were the inevitable third point of a triangle of hate, understood to be the hidden engineers and intended beneficiaries of all wrongdoing.

Although Federalism was largely based on urban centres, the issues of the summer of 1793 could also set light to continuing rural grievances. Smouldering resentments at wealthy beneficiaries of the sale of *biens nationaux*, discontent with new rules for the management of the vital local forests, and hostility to regicide and the expulsion of the Girondins were all expressed in short-lived insurrection in the eastern department of the Jura. Meanwhile in the neighbouring Doubs, fear of conscription blended with

previous page
Lesueur depictions of the vagaries of military volunteering - one man's self-designed uniform, that was not emulated, and a father stepping forward to take the place of his disabled son. (Musée Carnavalet).

rumours of invasion to spark an actual uprising of over 1,000 men, from communities that had been disaffected ever since the clerical oath. Montagnard repression brought over 500 arrests, and forty-three executions.

In the major cities, there was a superficial logic to the beliefs that now split republicans. The relatively wealthy and those impoverished enough to launch food riots were easy to see as essentially opposed. But the actual conduct of all concerned challenged a simple division. The defenders of Federalist Lyon, who held out under Jacobin siege until October, resolve under close scrutiny into a range of occupational groups remarkably similar to those who populated the Parisian *sans-culottes* movement over the same months. That movement itself proved strikingly flexible in regard to its short-term social agendas.

Paris was rocked in mid-July 1793 by the assassination of the firebrand journalist Marat at the hands of Charlotte Corday. This young Norman gentlewoman used her trial to condemn Marat's own (mythical) corruption, and proclaim the virtues of the Federalist cause, before going to the guillotine as a virgin martyr. In the wake of these events, several groups, including some ardent female activists, and a noted patriot priest, Jacques Roux, took up the mantle of a *Maratiste* stance, demanding harsh action against wealthy food hoarders, and further mobilization for the war effort.

With remarkable unanimity, those leading the established radical forces, including both Robespierre and Hébert, rounded on these groups in print and speeches as *enragés*, 'lunatics', whose destabilizing demands went too far. At a moment when the Convention still hoped to negotiate the peaceful return of the Federalist cities to the fold, the Montagnards and *sans-culottes* Cordelier groupings were willing to use almost-Girondin rhetoric against those further to their left. With remarkable hypocrisy, the Convention imposed the death penalty on hoarders, a key

NAYANT PU ME CORRO

ILS M'ONT ASSASSIN

enragé demand, at the end of July, just as these attacks ramped up. Jacques Roux was discredited, marginalized and later arrested as politically suspect. Female activists would be subjected to a blanket ban on public activities in the autumn.

As hopes of a quick Federalist surrender faded, Hébert and his *sans-culottes* colleagues shamelessly adopted the *enragé* agenda as their own. By mid-August, they pushed the Convention into passing a *levée en masse*, calling all able-bodied citizens into service appropriate to their age and sex, and requisitioning all the resources of the nation, from factories to carthorses, to the mission of national defence. Three weeks later, massive crowds were summoned by the *sans-culottes* leadership to demand further action from the Convention. In what was partly a showdown between the different radical leaderships, the Convention agreed a series of new laws. The blanket detention of 'suspect' individuals was imposed (and would eventually cover several hundred thousand people), and fears of food shortage were addressed with the creation of a 'General Maximum' system of price controls.

The latter, while causing moral convulsions among those in the Convention (including the Montagnard leadership) profoundly committed to economic free markets, was nothing less than a capitulation to popular demands for Old-Regime-style market regulation that had never gone away since 1789. But it was also accompanied by a far more contestable commitment to cutting wages back to pre-inflationary levels. *Sans-culottes* 'victories' on the Maximum and Law of Suspects were further counterweighted by a new limitation on local section meetings to twice a week, in a clear effort to block the power of a permanently mobilized Parisian movement. Throughout the Terror, everything that appeared to be a movement towards answering the demands of the common people always had another more compromised side.

The Death of Marat, 1793, squalor transformed into beauty by the brush of Jacques-Louis David.

Back in July 1793, the Convention had finally, almost a year after the fall of the monarchy, swept away all feudal dues without compensation, having the previous month also created a measure to sell *biens nationaux* in smaller blocks, and one that envisaged the possibility of the division of commons. But while these reached out to the more modest property owner, those who faced the continued piling of ex-feudal and ex-tithe burdens on their rents gained no relief. The summer saw rural unrest on this subject in departments from the Gers in the southwest to the Yonne, only a day's ride from Paris, but nobody in national politics saw any reason to raise it as a problem. Ordering Representatives-on-Mission in the same weeks to demolish fortified chateaux demonstrated clearly that in the Convention's mind, feudal lords and capitalist landlords had nothing in common.

*

Into the autumn of 1793, as a procession of leading royalist and Girondin figures passed under the guillotine in Paris, France continued to experience an astonishingly intense mixture of upheaval and mobilization. Representatives-on-Mission, who now criss-crossed the country in pairs by the dozen, burst repeatedly into local life. Sometimes animated by denunciatory correspondence received, sometimes relying on snap judgements about which groups looked or sounded more like true patriots, and often subject to manipulation by local factions on that score, they overthrew established local authorities, purged local Jacobins and other clubs, appointed new men as mayors and legal officials, and frequently conjured into life whole new ad hoc brigades of 'special commissioners' to pursue their purposes as they swept on elsewhere.

In a moment of fundamental economic disruption, the canny among the adult male population latched on to the ever-expanding waves of new bureaucracy for economic security and social influence. Every community since the spring had a 'surveillance committee' to manage the comings and goings of strangers, and issue 'civic certificates' to good patriots, without which life rapidly became impossible. The July hoarding ban, and the September Maximum, produced a need for literally tens of thousands of new postholders, all primed with intrusive powers that it was best to be seen to use zealously, or risk denunciation.

One appointed bureaucrat in the rural district of Cany, near Rouen, noted by the end of the year a tripartite division of the local population. The smallest group, but still to be found everywhere, were 'rich egoists' who needed to be watched carefully; outnumbering them, he recorded dutifully, were 'true sans-culottes', showing that the meaning of this word had already expanded far beyond its urban origins. But the largest group was 'the indifferent, of whom the countryside counts a great number, incapable of having an opinion of their own'.[37] It was the writer's thankless task to constantly prod such men into patriotic stances, which in all probability were simply meaningless to them.

Another September measure brought into existence *armées révolutionnaires* – not actual combat armies, but rather bands of urban *sans-culottes* activists, given weapons and uniforms with the specific mission of hunting down hoarding and 'incivic' conduct among the rural population. They were the ancient clash of cultures between food producers and urban consumers brought ferociously to life. Often sent out in small numbers to hostile communities, the *armées*, like the Representatives-on-Mission, made violent snap judgements about whom to believe and whom to denounce, roaring, as one typical charge did, about 'hoarders, men of the law, priests and agents of former nobles' on all sides.[38]

The *armées*' licence to use force encouraged them to play up to the *sans-culottes* stereotype to its full – many took pride in cultivating ferocious-looking whiskers, and many a village tavern was drunk dry by the *hommes à moustaches* as a base for their intimidating raids on local farmers and merchants. One result of such disruptive presences was a rise in overt criminality. In October 1793, isolated farmsteads around Corbeille, a day's ride south of Paris, were raided and pillaged by a twenty-five-strong gang, fully armed and in the uniforms of revolutionary troops – but they were mere robbers, and far from the only band operating in the region.

Another consequence was a stark rhetorical inflation of local politics into reflections of the national struggle. In the district of Lormes in the central department of the Nièvre, a passing Representative-on-Mission gave powers as a 'civil commissioner' to a man who nicknamed himself 'Marat' Chaix. Gathering together a small armed force, he proceeded to enforce state policies on requisitions and redistribution with a storm of abuse against the counter-revolutionary and corrupt ways of the local elite – he 'would rather be a dog', he said, than a bourgeois.[39] But Chaix was in fact a man previously elected as a local magistrate, and himself a comfortable landowner, who formed his armed gang with some of his own labourers. Whether he was overtaken by revolutionary enthusiasm, or an opportunist on the make, will never be entirely clear from the fog of denunciations that enfolded him, like so many at this moment.

In the small town of Gaillac, a day's ride east of Montauban, Benoît Lacombe was a young man from a noted middle-class family that in the 1780s had just made the leap to purchasing a noble title. He took a progressive stance on the Revolution that meshed with a pragmatic investment in *biens nationaux* that eventually amounted to over 250,000 *livres*, including the whole estate of the local abbey. In 1793 he was a leader of a local faction that called itself the '*sans-culottes* with pikes', modelled on the most militantly impoverished stereotype of plebeian mobilization.[40]

Purely local vendettas played a key role in at least some of the politics of the Terror. In the town of Tonnerre in the Yonne, two factions led by former land agents and bailiffs have been identified that fought out every battle of the decade between themselves, translating effortlessly into political terms an enmity which went back to the 1760s, and grouped many dozens of individuals on both sides. By mid-1793 they had dubbed themselves 'Montagnards' and '*sans-culottes*', and alternated between brawling in the streets and appealing to passing Representatives to favour one side or the other. Later in the year one faction's leadership fled to Paris under threat of arrest, succeeded in painting themselves as victimized patriots, and had the dispositions of the Representative responsible overturned in their favour. Fragile peace was imposed in this town of some 3,500 inhabitants by the detention of leaders on both sides in 1794.

If the agents of the Convention here appeared as umpires adjudicating the game of local politics, in other places the zeal of local activists could easily end up embroiling the Representatives themselves in their struggles. From the small town of Agde in the Hérault, one radical club denounced the Representative Joseph Boisset 'to the Mountain which had chosen you to be the exterminating angel of those bastards whom you are openly favouring and whom you are stirring up, even against us'.[41] Whatever the truth about the identity, social or political, of the bastards in question, Boisset was recalled and replaced a few months later.

However we think about the radicalizing dynamic of 1793, it took on multiplying new forms. The overt commitment of the Vendéen rebels to the cause of the Catholic religion produced in these months a wave of radical attacks on the practices of religion itself. Constitutional priests who had weathered all the previous storms of dissent now found themselves assailed: Parisian *sans-culottes* drove the archbishop of Paris into renouncing his vows, and took over the cathedral of Notre Dame to hold a blasphemous 'festival of reason'. Local ultra-revolutionaries in several regions took to publicly mocking the concept of the supernatural, conducting burlesque parodies of religious rites, defrocking priests, and even compelling them into marriage (ideally to former nuns).

A great deal of this was the crude anti-clericalism of hard-drinking urban artisans brought to violent life, but it also had an intellectual dimension. The Representative who had appointed Chaix, the former schoolteacher Joseph Fouché, used the Nièvre as a testbed for his emergent secularist ideas. Cemeteries, for example, were rebranded with signage declaring that 'Death is an eternal sleep' rather than a gateway to paradise or damnation. While Fouché moved on to supervise the savage repression of revolt in Lyon, other leaders brought to the Convention proposals to liberate France from the mental bondage of religious thinking.

On 20 September, Gilbert Romme, another former teacher, proposed to the Convention that the Gregorian calendar was, in itself, a set of shackles, weighted with 'the errors that credulity and superstitious routine have transmitted to us from centuries of ignorance'.[42] The passage of time was strongly marked by the liturgical calendar of the church – not only in enforced Sunday worship, but in the eating of fish rather than meat on Fridays, respecting Lent and Advent as seasons of fasting (when, for example, no marriages were performed), and in the fact that there were up to another fifty days a year marked for observance as religious holidays.

Romme instead proposed a calendar of twelve thirty-day months, with a five- or six-day exceptional period at the autumnal equinox to celebrate the founding of the Republic, and a strictly limited diet of festivals every ten days. After this was approved, another intellectual, Fabre d'Eglantine, added a layer of poetic nomenclature, based around seasonal weather conditions, to the months. From the end of October 1793, France found itself in Brumaire (the foggy month) of Year II of the Republic.

Imposition of the calendar accompanied a wave of other forms of renaming that had already begun in some radical centres, but now accelerated nationwide. Parisian sections with 'royalist' names had since 1792 swapped them for the more prosaic – Palais-Royal became Butte-des-Moulins (Mill Hill), Louvre, Muséum – or the more heroic: Henri IV, named after his statue on the Pont Neuf, became Révolutionnaire, while Luxembourg, named for a palace, became Mutius Scaevola, a mythical Roman general who burnt his own hand in a brazier to defy a threat of torture.

Once attention turned to religion, the ubiquity of saints' names in local geographies brought about a drastic overturning, especially in areas of intense conflict. Villages and towns west of Lyon recaptured from local 'Federalists', for example, were renamed systematically: Montbrison as Montbrisé ('mount broken', after its crushed resistance), Sainte-Polgues as Roche-Libre ('free rock'), Saint-Haon-le-Châtel as Bel-Air ('good air'), Saint-Just-en-Chevalet as Montmarat.

While such sweeping moves pleased those who thought they marked the milestones of political regeneration, others even among the patriot elite were not so sure. The same official in Cany who had complained of the massive numbers of the 'indifferent' reported that, by the spring of 1794, renaming had become a 'disorderly mania' among local communities, who 'abandon insignificant names only to take on others even more insignificant'.[43] One hidden problem of this trend was the disruption to rural postal services, which years later were still perplexed by the instability of addresses, and the lack of any central registers. For those who sought to challenge, rather than discreetly lament, such practices, and especially for those who did so in the name of religion, the consequences were deadly.

Slaughter and
Reaction

By the time the 'dechristianizers' set fully to work, the war in the Vendée had been raging for six months. It was a war of manoeuvres and skirmishes, of rebel columns failing to take major towns, and republican columns failing to pin down rebels in the *bocage* countryside, criss-crossed with impenetrable ancient hedgerows. Fury and frustrations on both sides continued to erupt in massacre. On the rebel side, leadership passed gradually from local ad hoc groups to more established noble figures – sometimes pressed into service against their first inclinations by ardent rank-and-file demands. The sense of such men that the 'Royal and Catholic Army' should be held together as a conventional force with conventional goals of meeting the enemy in open battle, rather than dispersing to fight as guerrillas, would help bring it to its doom.

On the republican side, the summer months were dominated by the interventions of the Parisian *sans-culottes* movement. Having taken control of the central War Ministry through political machinations, Cordeliers radicals appointed generals to lead the campaign on the basis of their loyalties and social identities, rather than their competencies. One such, Rossignol, was so violently and drunkenly incompetent that his existence provoked disputes with Representatives-on-Mission that actively contributed to the collapse into factional fratricide that emerged in 1794.

Incompetent leadership, coupled with the amateurish soldiering of *sans-culottes* National Guards and volunteers, helped to produce the series of setbacks and reverses that translated easily into betrayals and panics, driving up the tendency for such forces to resort to retaliatory massacres. From August 1793 onwards the Convention began to direct more regular military forces into the region, and impose some order on their leadership. The resultant campaign, as the Vendéens first attempted to secure a major urban base, then tried to fight their way to the coast of

Normandy, expecting British support that failed to arrive, turned by the late autumn increasingly to flight and slaughter.

In October the Convention spokesman Bertrand Barère described all the rebels 'from the age of ten to sixty-six' as 'brigands', with their womenfolk as 'scouts', and concluded that 'the whole population of this revolted land is in armed rebellion' – a fact which, from the legislation of the previous March, condemned them to death. The Royal and Catholic Army, with its women and children, as much as 100,000 strong, was brought to bay at Savenay on the north bank of the Loire estuary on 23 December 1793. General Westermann reported proudly to the Convention that 'I have crushed children beneath my horses' hooves, and massacred the women, who thus will give birth to no more brigands... We take no prisoners, they would need to be given the bread of liberty, and pity is not revolutionary.'[44]

The impact of such horrific imagery can be tempered by observing that leaders such as Westermann were under intense pressure to demonstrate their commitment to the Republic rhetorically, in the knowledge that dozens of other senior officers were under arrest, and some had already been guillotined as counter-revolutionaries for their failings. But the carnage inflicted on the Vendée was also very real, and would extend through the winter months as another professional general, Turreau, launched *colonnes infernales*, 'hell columns', through the core rebel territories, exterminating populations that were taken axiomatically to be enemy brigands.

One village, Montbert in the Loire-Inférieure, had lost eleven men fighting for the rebel armies in 1793. On 11 February 1794, a hell column swept through the village and slaughtered seventy-two people, including forty-nine women. Two weeks later, another column killed six more men and fourteen more women. Over the coming months, patrols returned again and again,

overleaf
A melodramatic nineteenth-century depiction of the
Vendéen rebellion in its later, most martial stages.
(*Battle of Le Mans*, Jean Sorieul, 1852)

catching the terrified inhabitants by handfuls. Men were shot where they stood, women taken off into a nearby forest, and later found clustered together in death. More than 175 killings were recorded, and like many other places in this ravaged land, the survivors were struck by epidemic diseases that killed almost as many.

A final accounting of casualties will never be known, but estimates suggest that, including the death toll from unchecked disease, up to 250,000 rebels and other locals perished, alongside as many as 100,000 on the republican side. The Vendée was only one dimension of the civil war that 'the Terror' confronted. Up and down the Rhône valley and its flanking highlands, Federalism merged with pre-existing sectarian conflict and the active incitement of émigrés to the east to produce hectic and savage fighting.

Lyon and Marseille were regained for the Republic by early autumn, but the latter's defenders fled to the naval port of Toulon, where they satisfied every *sans-culottes* paranoid fantasy by inviting in the British Royal Navy and an émigré contingent to help protect them from Jacobin revenge (gifting them France's Mediterranean fleet in the process). A siege that continued into mid-December ensued, until the young artillery officer Napoleon Bonaparte led a breakthrough assault on a fortress that commanded the harbour, and propelled the British into a hasty evacuation, leaving the locals to their fate.

Toulon, like Lyon, Marseille and other recaptured centres, was subjected to the rigours of revolutionary justice, as special tribunals dealt death to rebels condemned out of hand. Across the country there were thousands of such executions, perhaps as many as 30,000–40,000 if every process of summary judgment is included. Jacobin rhetoric continued to insist on the leadership of the selfish social elite in rebellion, but had also taken an almost-racial tinge of disparagement – one Representative declared of

Lyon in October that 'one is stupid here by temperament', blaming fogs from the river for 'thickening' minds.[45]

Towards the end of the year a second group of Representatives, sent to intensify Lyon's repression, declared that 'there are no innocent men in this city', except those actually locked up by the Federalists.[46] Revolutionary justice eventually despatched 1,800 people, perhaps 1.5 per cent of the whole population. In Toulon, 800 were executed. In each location, the list of actual victims demonstrated the cross-class nature of resistance. In Marseille, eighteen wholesale merchants, ten lawyers and forty-two assorted property owners were executed, but also three bakers, three butchers, one carpenter, eleven clerks, eighteen farmers and market gardeners, two hatters, one news hawker, five shoemakers, three tailors and one journeyman sweetmaker.

Brutal mass executions were the extreme end of experiences of this period, but the mobilizations of the 'Terror' reached into every corner of France. Communities wise or compliant enough to simply knuckle down under the authority of Representatives and civil commissioners still found themselves hounded to produce men, crops and military supplies of all kinds in vast and unreasonable quantities. To feed the population under violently disrupted conditions, rationing was widely imposed, even as productive areas were also compelled to ship their grains to the towns, and to accept maximum prices for them.

Knuckling down itself became harder, as more active acceptance of ever more intrusive republican ideology was demanded, and officials, closely watched by others for signs of backsliding, responded to dissent with hair-trigger denunciations of counter-revolutionary intent. Even for those who retained a sense of genuine patriotic commitment, the sheer mechanical effort of trying to deal with what was expected from Paris became impossible. In the last month of 1793 alone, the national authorities sent out 300 separate administrative orders to all

localities, in thirteen bundles – a tidal wave of paper that for many overwhelmed all reason.

Precisely how most countryfolk reacted to all this we cannot know, because the profoundly dangerous consequences of speaking out were clear to all, and only the denunciation of such dissent produced written records. In the winter of 1793–4, one poor sharecropper in the Périgord, Jean Bernard, found himself on trial after a grumpy conversation about the worthlessness of the *assignats* prompted him to take down some of the official notices posted on the local church door, saying 'I need some nails to fix my clogs, and some paper to wipe my ----', as the record delicately put it.[47] His fate is unknown, but there were hundreds, perhaps thousands of such trials of disgruntled peasants during the Terror.

The arbitrary way in which they were treated is signalled by the fate of peasant brother and sister Léonard and Paule Meynard, from the village of Romain-sur-Colle, in the Dordogne. A banal squabble with a local official, in which they grabbed some papers from his hands, expressing frustration and disgust with the burden of republican demands, sent them all the way to the Revolutionary Tribunal in Paris, and the guillotine, ten days before Robespierre's fall. It was sometimes wiser to express one's views without words, as the female inhabitants of Saint-Vincent in the Haute-Loire did one day in June 1794. Commanded to attend the local church so that an official could give an oration on the Supreme Being, they rose as he began to speak, turned and presented him with their bared buttocks, setting off a short-lived, but unanswerable, local trend.

*

If we choose to see the underlying reality of the 'Terror', beginning with the demands for conscripts that triggered the Vendéen revolt, and extending through the purges of all those perceived

The siege of Toulon, in an idealised bird's-eye view.
(Jean-Antoine-Siméon Fort, 1842)

to be hindering an effort of national defence, as essentially a war emergency, then one thing which must be acknowledged about it, on the overall level, is that it worked. By the end of 1793, all those areas of the country that had fallen out of central control were, one way or another, back in the fold – or at least their resistance was suppressed to no more than nuisance level.

Thanks to the *levée en masse*, and to the huge energizing efforts of Representatives around the country, France was on the way to raising an army of 800,000 men, twice the size of any it had raised before, and managing – just barely, but extraordinarily nonetheless – to clothe and arm them and have them ready for battle. Republican ideology, which had slashed so many with its razor-sharp edges, was also proving to be a potent engine of individual commitment and self-sacrifice.

A blizzard of propaganda speeches, public displays, theatrical productions, and literally hundreds of thousands of pamphlets and newspapers swirled around the conscripts of 1793, and found echo in their own sentiments in letters home. One Pierre Cohin wrote from the northern front that their war was 'the war of liberty against despotism. There can be no doubt that we shall be victorious. A nation that is just and free is invincible.' Gabriel Bourguignon, from the Indre, wrote home that he 'would rather die a hundred times over than concede an inch to the enemy', and he and his comrades would defend their just cause 'to the very last drop of our blood'.[48]

'Liberty, Equality, Fraternity, or Death!' was no empty slogan when troops hurled themselves time and again at enemy lines in 1794, and achieved staggering breakthroughs. François-Xavier Joliclerc, a volunteer from a village in the eastern Jura, had written to his parents to have no regrets at his departure for the front lines, they should instead rejoice, for 'either you will see me return bathed in glory, or you will have a son who is a worthy citizen of France who knows how to die for the defence of his

An example of republican iconography, drawing heavily on ancient Roman inspiration, produced by the Tremblay firm, original publishers of Hébert's *Père Duchesne*.

LIBERTÉ
EGALITÉ
FRATERNITÉ
OU LA MORT

UNITÉ
INDIVISIBILITÉ
DE LA
RÉPUBLIQUE

De l'Imprimerie de TREMBLAY, rue basse

country'.[49] Such purity of intention was perhaps easy to sustain in the ranks – certainly once victories began to flow – but it was harder to translate into the complexities of civilian life.

Jacobin, 'terrorist' republicanism, spawned out of the betrayals of every other set of political leaders since 1789, consumed itself through its obsession with transparent political virtue, a quality almost impossible to manifest in practice. It left behind in the summer of 1794 a motley crew of political survivors, among whom were many who had been active persecutors of dissent among the common people barely months before. It also left behind an ardent rhetoric that associated the most disruptive elements of 'terrorist' practice with the common people and their supposed *sans-culottes* avatars. This meant that, while 'terrorism' had brought suffering to France in many ways, the 'anti-terrorism' of the Thermidorian era would be little better for most of those struggling to survive in a near-shattered country.

*

It has long been commonplace to associate the 'Terror' with a commitment to social justice, and the 'Thermidorian reaction' with a return to conservative oligarchy – and this is an argument both left and right can turn to their favour, depending on what they seek to preach. The truth is, as ever, more complex. The Montagnards did propose, in their 1794 Ventôse Decrees, to redistribute confiscated land to 'poor patriots', but they never succeeded in doing so, or even defining who such 'poor patriots' would be. It is easy to suspect that in practice many would have been the pushy conformists who took up so many other benefits of power at this moment.

The Montagnards also set up a few months later a 'Grand Register of National Welfare' which made some limited payments to widows and the elderly, but this was a skeletal replacement for religious charity at best. Such schemes sat within a wider imagined structure of future life which plotted a control over the people's thoughts and deeds as thorough as anything the dechristianizers accused the church of exercising. Indeed, in the 'Cult of the Supreme Being', launched with massive festivities in early June 1794, Robespierre and his associates looked to integrate the explicit power of supernatural divinity to reinforce the didactic messages of the new calendar's parade of celebrations.

They also presided over a system that crushed dissent from below ruthlessly. The *sans-culottes* movement, for all its flaws, did keep in touch with the feelings of its Parisian base, and one reason for the tensions which led to its elimination in the spring of 1794 was discontent at the working of the maximum price system. Black-marketeering flourished, and Parisian crowds in February and March 1794 had flared into protest – for the third time in as many years – at prices of butter, eggs and other goods, unavailable without paying illegal amounts. The Montagnard answer was to increase the legal prices, while also, incomprehensibly, to start planning for an enforced downward revision in wage rates, as if that would somehow create a new equilibrium.

By April, resultant workers' protests were being banned using the laws established under the monarchy in 1791, and ringleaders of movements among bakers, plasterers, tobacco workers and others were arrested as dangerous subversives. The many thousands who worked in the new war industries of the capital, and in manufactories dispersed across the nation, were effectively under military discipline, and compelled to take wages that left them reliant on state rations.

Emblematic of the Montagnards' attitudes to work and workers was the enforcement of the Republican Calendar itself, with its most direct material consequence: nine-day uninterrupted stretches of labour between single days of *décadi* 'rest' (often accompanied by compulsory festive participation). The Catholic calendar of feasts and Sundays had given workers around a

overleaf
A mid-nineteenth-century depiction of the moment the National Convention turned against Robespierre.
(*The Ninth of Thermidor*, Raymond Quinsac Monvoisin, c. 1840).

hundred rest days a year (roughly equivalent to modern two-day weekends); the Jacobin Republic expected them to manage with barely forty.

Robespierre and his colleagues went to the guillotine in late July amid a renewed storm of popular protest at a further effort to crack down on wages. Crowds cursed the '*foutu* Maximum', and were rewarded two weeks later with new wage scales up to 50 per cent higher. But prices were also pushed up substantially in October, and on 24 December 1794 the new authorities signalled a dramatic change of direction, abandoning price controls altogether.

This shift was emblematic of a regime that was finding its political footing most secure when it leant rightwards, rehabilitating the Girondins, liberating many counter-revolutionary suspects and treating Montagnard economic policies as the outcome of illegitimate blackmail by the *sans-culottes* movement, to whom the label 'terrorist' was first applied in earnest in these months.

The Thermidorians continued to provide bread and meat rations to the cities, though in shrinking and eventually pitiful amounts, but the end of the Maximum was undoubtedly a measure of callous indifference, if overlaid with the prevalent idiotic optimism about the naturally self-righting nature of markets. It failed to reckon with the absolutely profound economic disruption of the previous two years of civil war and emergency mobilization, with the inflation that had rendered the *assignat* currency almost meaningless, and with the continued wartime blockade.

Above all, though, it coincided with the onset of a winter every bit as ferocious as the one that had greeted 1789. Farmers' planting had already been cut back by the general disruption, and unwillingness to grow a surplus likely to be confiscated by the 'terrorists'; then autumn rains had wrecked a proportion of what existed; now a massive freeze set in, blocking road and river transportation. The result was a quite literal famine.

Exacerbated by a further desperate shortage of firewood, town and country alike suffered monstrously. Suicides became so common in Paris that the authorities suppressed news of them to avert panic. In the ice-bound northern regions, old people reportedly simply walked out into the fields to die. Infants found no milk at starving mothers' breasts. The recorded death rate in Rouen doubled by midwinter, and more than doubled again into the second half of 1795, as long-term malnutrition carried off the already weakened. Across the country for the next year or more, the birth rate plummeted as chronic hunger disrupted female fertility.

As winter passed into spring, some aspects of the situation only grew worse. Bread rations in Paris had been cut back to less than half a pound a day, and workers had to buy more with *assignats* worth less than 10 per cent of their face value. Bread on the open market had cost ten times its long-term price in March 1795, by May it had soared to 150 times that price. At this point, the sense of this as a price anyone except the rich could imagine paying simply evaporates. Parisians had already had enough.

Uncoordinated marches and protests in March coalesced in early April into a general crowd invasion of the Convention, demanding 'Bread and the Constitution of 1793' – the totemic democratic document the Montagnards had suspended 'until the peace' (which had yet to come). Easily dispersed by military force, and lacking any agenda except a desperate plea for republican solidarity, Parisians suffered through a further six weeks of shortages before renewed desperation led to an initially more threatening mobilization, and one which took the life, and head, of a Convention deputy as he tried to bar their progress into the Convention's hall.

Lacking any sense of an alternative power structure to replace the Convention, which remained idolized in radical rhetoric, this 'Prairial rising', last gasp of a *sans-culottes* sensibility, melted away as the authorities rallied resistance. It served to conveniently incriminate some surviving more radical Montagnards, who now suffered a fatal purge, along with the remnants of the *sans-culottes* movement in the Parisian sections.

Across the country at large, the effort to deal with the 'terrorists' crossed over with a movement of overt counter-revolutionary revenge, a 'White Terror' that saw several spectacular massacres in centres along the Rhône valley. While this killed hundreds, the compulsory denunciation of 'terrorists' saw as many as 100,000 arrested, imprisoned, and often sentenced to the 'civil death' of 'disarmament' – marked out as untrustworthy to hold the duties of a citizen.

These processes condemned some to persecutions that would endure until their deaths – in some cases, after decades of scorn and marginalization – but others managed to slip through the net. 'Marat' Chaix, who had terrorized Lormes in 1793, was arrested by Montagnard agents as part of the purge of 'Hébertists' in early 1794, but found freedom after Thermidor to resume his landowning lifestyle, and was unafraid to defend himself in correspondence when challenged. In other areas, those who had worn a conformist mask of radicalism even more lightly found it easy to slip off and begin preaching the values of law and order. That, above all, was what authorities would spend the rest of the decade seeking, but those years were to show how deeply many months of factional conflict had scarred France, and how hard it remained to deliver any of the promises of 1789.

A satire from 1796 by the engraver Joseph Hunin on the proliferation of high-value *assignat* bills in Thermidorian France, resulting, as the central figure depicts, only in beggary.

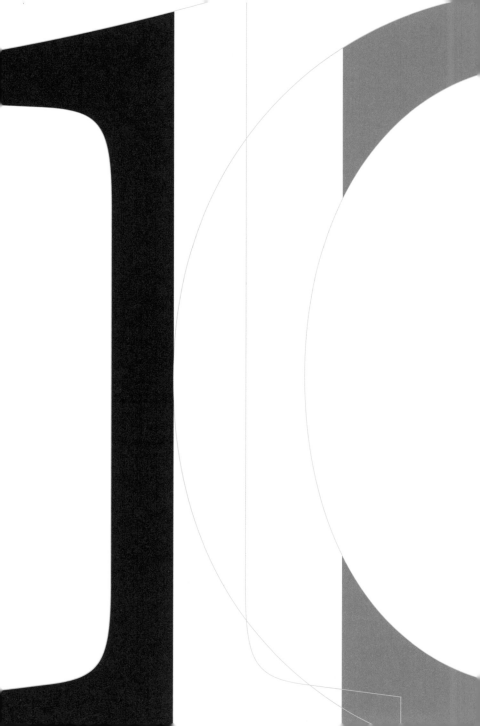

Moving On,
Looking Back

The Thermidorian Convention drew up a new constitution in the summer of 1795, and put it into operation in the autumn. It was, on the one hand, a model of rational, balanced institution-building, and on the other, a grotesque fudge. It created a two-chamber legislature and a deliberately distributed executive power, with a five-man 'Directory' occupying the role of a presidency overseeing actual ministers. Annual elections on a taxpayer franchise would renew the legislators regularly, who would themselves choose the 'Directors' for rotating terms, so no single power bloc could perpetuate itself. All this, however, was imposed with a law that two-thirds of the new legislative seats were to be occupied initially by members of the existing Convention, because they did not trust the country to elect the right people.

The actual basis of support for this liberal structure was terrifyingly narrow. A right-wing, increasingly 'royalist' opposition in Paris itself raised an insurrection in October 1795 against this attempt to shut them out, and had to be driven off by troops under general Bonaparte. Scant weeks later, left-wing forces in the capital began rallying around a former feudal lawyer, 'Gracchus' Babeuf, who through the winter and spring developed increasingly elaborate plans for a radical coup d'état until rounded up in May 1796.

Once regular annual elections were properly instituted from 1797, each successive round saw stark interference from the state, acting to counterbalance 'dangerous' swings to left or right. With disruption of assemblies, nullification of results and dozens of political arrests, these events themselves were widely understood as coups by the government against the electorate.

Blatant force, often in military hands, was the first and last resort of the Directorial Republic. Its very birth depended on the fact of the Terror's military triumph, bequeathing a vast and combat-hardened army that in 1794–5 had cascaded into the

Netherlands and the Rhineland, subjugating the Dutch Republic and extorting favourable peace with Prussia. It punched so hard across the Pyrenees that the cowed Spanish were propelled into changing sides against Britain in 1796. In that year and the next, general Bonaparte led an army into Italy that battered Austria into submission, leaving only a naval war with Britain and a distant threat from Russia to justify continued mobilization.

The establishment of a strong and expanded French Republic (absorbing Belgium, the Rhineland and Alpine lands directly), and subservient 'sister republics' from Holland to the Po Valley, gave the Directory legitimacy it could not otherwise claim on its internal record. It also, and perhaps even more decisively, allowed its armies to be maintained on other territories at the expense of their inhabitants, and produced a stream of outright loot into the French treasury which counterbalanced fiscal and financial collapse at home.

The abandonment of the Terror's controls on prices had reignited the ferocious inflation of the *assignat* paper currency. As it tumbled in value, the Directory demonstrated its social sympathies clearly by prohibiting the early repayment of loans with devalued paper, and allowing landlords to demand half their rents in kind. It also sought to have half of the land tax paid the same way, though in what was by now a well-established practice almost nobody bothered to pay. In one month alone in late 1795, the state's printers ran off 800 million *livres* in face-value currency, and a threatened strike by the print workers nearly caused its own political crisis. The *assignats* had originally been intended to cover a national debt of around a billion *livres*. By the end of 1795, over 45 billion *livres* had been printed.

While the state could thrust wads of paper in the direction of those to whom it owed money, all this chaos left ordinary people reduced to barter, or haggling over a dwindling supply of small change. The problem persisted for years. A new currency, the *mandat territorial*, supposedly fixed against the value of land, was introduced in March 1796, crashed out of its 'fixed' value in July, and was abandoned having inflated to worthlessness in February 1797. Recovery eventually came by way of reintroduction of some of the Old Regime's most hated taxes, those on objects and transactions that could not be avoided, including by 1798 a special tobacco tax, and by the very thing the Revolution had erupted to avoid: an effective state bankruptcy, as two-thirds of its debts were transferred into new bonds whose value proved immediately evanescent.

The general economic picture of these years is equally chaotic. Colonial and other overseas trade, the mainstay of much economic growth in the previous century, was paralysed by naval blockade, and captive markets in the 'sister republics' could only compensate a little. Whole regions where the textile trade had given work to both towns and villages lay sometimes in literal ruins, and elsewhere merely economically devastated – across France, numbers of active weaving looms struggled to reach a half or even a third of their pre-1789 level. The Directory promoted high-level scientific and technological innovation through new state-funded elite institutes, but translating it into new industries ran into the twin blockages of a drought of capital and a revolutionary machine-breaking Luddism against threats to handcraft.

Life for ordinary peasants in these years ground on, as villagers navigated between the realities of chaotic breakdown and the almost hallucinatory structures of republican culture. At the level of the individual community, the relentless work of agriculture continued, and so too in many places did the entirely local politics of families, clans and vendettas. One study of six widely differing village communities through this period illustrates the possibilities of the era.

In two southern villages, Roquelaure (near Toulouse) and

Allan (north of Marseille), a landholding village elite that had held office before 1789 continued to monopolize it throughout the 1790s, following the national trends in forming and disbanding committees and societies, and shifting rhetorical strategies, but with always the same family names running through the records. There is no evidence of any groundswell of opposition from their poorer neighbours. Solidarity in Allan may have been reinforced by a persistent legal vendetta against their local (ex-)seigneur, a battle that had begun in 1785 and dragged on through six separate processes until 1818.[50]

Two other villages, Châtelaudren in northern Brittany and Saint-Alban on the southern slopes of the Massif Central, were dominated by their local legal and mercantile classes. The Breton community, relatively undivided, seems to have eased through the traumas of the decade with little material disruption. Saint-Alban, however, was riven by factional rivalries between families enmeshed in the management of seigneurial rights and properties. An undated petition from their poorer neighbours during the Terror lamented that 'agents of the old regime… seek to reproduce themselves under new forms and vex us more than ever'.

Representatives-on-Mission found evidence of systematic fraud and malpractice in both political and financial matters, and arrests were made, but in the turbulent politics of the time it seems charges were not made to stick. Higher authorities in 1796 noted that any information emerging from the village had to be treated carefully, on account of its 'inveterate and profound hatreds which have often produced factious outbursts'. Such conflict did not prevent the riven elite maintaining control, with the same family names appearing in office well into the next century.[51]

The village of Neuviller in Lorraine was threatened with a similar factional conflict early in the 1790s, when the local priest and new municipality were at loggerheads, but the former's emigration seems to have calmed matters, and local landowners and master craftsmen navigated the shoals of the Terror successfully, helped by some strategic redistribution of common lands to the poor. The final village of the six, Villepreux near Versailles, was the only one to see dramatic social changes. Initially dominated by wealthy tenant farmers and wholesalers, waves of elections in 1790 and 1791 steadily lowered the average wealth of office holders, until at the end of 1792 the elite was completely displaced by the local craftworkers (with one token farmer as mayor).

Changes that elsewhere were rhetorical here saw real shifts in personnel – in early 1793 the new surveillance committee incorporated wage workers alongside craftsmen. Working with the leadership of the Versailles district, such figures even managed to map out a redistribution scheme for former royal lands in 1794, although the proposed one-acre plots were more like gardens than viable farms. All this, however, did not survive post-Thermidorian national trends, and by the later 1790s some of the original taxpaying elite had been returned to power, alongside others who had profited from the wider sell-off of royal lands.[52]

Even as communities worked their way back to stability, in a landholding world that thought in generations rather than years, they were still beholden to the centralizing republican vision of transformation. The new calendar continued to be enforced (although 'the liberty of cults' was proclaimed for private worship), and alongside it the metric system, introduced in 1795, demanded yet another mental slate-wiping. All time-honoured local and regional understandings of distance, area, weight and volume – so critical for hard-fought battles over who owed what from the crop, and who owned what on the land – were erased. Of course in practice, in the heads of people who needed to think about these things every day, they continued in use, opening up another gulf between state and people.

Perhaps the widest chasm that grew in these years was between the Republic's claim that France was 'The Great Nation', resuming its role on the world stage, and the reality of the breakdown of law, order and public safety across the land. The French armies may have been vast and victorious, but they also lacked any mechanism to discharge the men swept up in the great recruitments of 1793, or (until the very end of the century) any system to replace them. Men in the ranks often found themselves suffering horribly. The proud patriotic volunteer Joliclerc wrote to his mother in February 1796, from his post fighting Breton guerrillas, that 'a pound and a half of poor-quality rye bread' was their daily ration, and 'the majority of soldiers are barefoot'. He pleaded with her to send help, or see him 'die in misery'.[53]

Joliclerc was wounded in action shortly after, and able on that basis to escape legitimately to his home, where he lived another thirty-six years. Other soldiers, like those who followed Napoleon into Italy, had their poverty relieved by the loot of campaigning. But these were only ever a minority. The French armies were thus plagued with desertion, and those deserters forced to live outside the law. When regular conscription did begin in 1799, and into the next decade, there were huge areas of the country, especially in the centre, west and southwest, where at least a third, and in some regions up to two-thirds, of those summoned to serve refused to go.

Many deserters, like those who had evaded the original drafts, lived with tacit or active family and community support; but even these were at constant risk of denunciation. Those lacking such shelter drifted in several directions. One was into overt counter-revolutionary brigandage. Across northwestern France the memory of the Vendée and of the wider *Chouan* guerrilla movements in Brittany and Normandy was revived as the Terror relented, and active combat drew in enormous republican forces (over 100,000 men in the winter of 1795–6) that crushed a second attempt at a full-blown rising. Sporadic conflict remained endemic here, however, and was echoed in the southeast, where royalist brigand gangs raided a swathe of towns from Saint-Etienne to Montpellier in the same months.

Other deserters swelled the ranks of violent criminals, joining those also driven to crime by the collapse of both the economy and charitable relief. The later 1790s would long be remembered by communities as a time when fear stalked the countryside. Some bands clung to a veneer of anti-republican principle: mail coaches were robbed of public funds in transit, leaving private citizens unharmed, public granaries were raided in the Aisne, prominent purchasers of *biens nationaux* were singled out for extortion, or as for example in the Drôme in 1796–7, 'disarmed' in a parody of official condemnations. Such selectivity helped to avoid too much local hostility to the perpetrators, reflecting the extent to which the republican elite had isolated itself from the mass of the people.

Just as common, however, was violent crime that offered no selective justification for its brutality. In the northern region of Picardy, farmers lived in fear of the *sommation minatoire*, intimidatory extortion letters threatening arson and pillage. Across a whole swathe of neighbouring areas, gangs became known for the practice of *chauffage*, 'warming' victims' feet in their fires until they revealed their hidden valuables. Some of these bands swelled into virtual private armies. The *Bande de Salembrier* roamed the northern border region with over sixty participants in 1795–7. The *Bande d'Orgères* numbered over 120, and terrorized the Eure-et-Loir department south of Paris until finally hunted down in 1799, having at its peak in 1796–7 been raiding farms at the rate of more than one a week. Over seventy-five murders, including several outright massacres of whole households, were charged to them.

Law and order in these years had broken down not just practically but also conceptually. The idea of relatively neutral 'authorities' who could be relied on to uphold a generally understood framework of law, even if at the cost of legal wrangling and expensive appeals, was destroyed by the events of 1789. In the early years of the Revolution it had seemed simple, if arduous, to merely replace the old order with a new one. A combination of counter-revolutionary plotting – real and perceived – and the resistance of the population to legal, but unacceptable, demands over feudalism had cracked that new framework.

By 1792–3 institutional neutrality was increasingly being replaced by the demands of political loyalty. That in itself often concealed a system-shattering reality of local factionalism, opportunism and self-interested vendetta, that spiralled into murderous denunciation, and sometimes outright murder, into the Terror and out the other side. By 1795, therefore, those who held local power and legal offices in France were largely those who had either come out on top in vicious power struggles, or who had cunningly ridden the various waves of national politics while cynically safeguarding their own interests. They were certainly not men committed to applying the rule of law, especially not to their own disadvantage.

If villages like Saint-Alban and Villepreux managed to confine conflict and change to elections and rhetoric, others like the small agricultural town of Aubagne, near Marseille, saw cold-blooded factional murder committed in public. The killing of three local Jacobin militants in June 1795 – beaten into near-unrecognizability, shot multiple times and mutilated – was followed by a three-year spree of violence and intimidation involving over forty murders, robberies and assaults, for which,

overleaf
The Revolution Ends: the final implosion of constitutional order, as Napoleon Bonaparte jostles with angry legislators during his November 1799 coup.
(*Bonaparte and the Council of 500 at St-Cloud, François Bouchot, 1840*)

eventually, no fewer than sixty-seven people were tried; but not until an entirely new regime had taken power.[54]

Just as national politics dissolved into an eternal round of coups defying the will of an increasingly polarized electorate, so local administration, and local justice, ran at the whim of those in charge, and so others increasingly resorted to extra-legal means to protect themselves and further their own interests. All of these strains ultimately came together in 1799 in a lurch towards strong, authoritarian government. Facing a crisis born of military overstretch in the Mediterranean and a revived counter-revolutionary alliance, with Austria once again in the field and French armies driven out of Italy, the country tottered. Conscription introduced the previous year sparked riots in several regions, shading over towards renewed royalist and Catholic insurrection.

The electorate, the legislature and the Directory were at loggerheads, and even the plot of November 1799 that created a 'Consulate' government and put Napoleon Bonaparte at its head only barely succeeded in avoiding a vigorous riposte from outraged deputies. Once in place, however, a government led by a general began to reintroduce law and order at the point of a bayonet. The tactics of flying columns and summary execution applied to rebels were turned on bandits, and as they slowly restored a semblance of normality, so top-down processes of administrative renewal offered an end to local strife, at the cost of submission.

Revived military success, with a second crushing of Austria, and even Britain brought to the peace table by 1801, cemented a sense of returning stability seen elsewhere in a swathe of moves, from a return to metal currency to a formal reconciliation with the Catholic Church, and even a quiet acceptance of returning émigré nobles, as long as they behaved themselves. Future years of renewed and ever more arduous war would show that submitting to Bonaparte's megalomaniac ambition had been a devil's bargain, but after a decade of unremitting strife, so often promoted in the name of the people's liberty, it is hard to blame the French for yearning for the stability of the iron fist.

Epilogue:
A Final Reckoning

During the years of internal peace that Napoleonic rule brought (whatever its other tragic demands in sacrifice), the French peasantry was able at last to consolidate the gains it had sought ever since the *cahiers* of 1789. Feudal dues had passed into oblivion in 1793, and while the heaping of dues and tithes on to rents was a persistent grievance, years of conscription produced labour shortages that shifted the balance of power towards tenants, easing their long-term burdens. Peasants also gained, eventually, from the sale of *biens nationaux*, which ultimately saw around a tenth of all land change hands, two-thirds from the church and the remainder from confiscated royal and émigré properties.

The Thermidorians, desperate for cash, had added to the short-term inequity of the market by abandoning auction sales in 1795 for disposal to anyone who could put down seventy-five times the assessed annual yield of agricultural property, in face-value paper. This boon to the holders of large quantities of inflated *assignats* nonetheless left many of these wanting to sell on parcels of land later to realize their profits. Earlier rounds of accumulation also produced later divisions and re-sales, in a shuffling process that ultimately saw around 500,000 individual purchasers – perhaps one in ten of all households.

Peasant land ownership rose from under 45 per cent of all land to around a half, although patterns of ownership continued to vary widely. In the Seine-et-Oise near Paris, the pressure to produce for the urban market kept large farms dominant, and peasant owners only secured around one-eighth of the land that changed hands; things were little better near other major cities. In the densely populated Nord, however, where rural populations had been swollen by pre-revolutionary cottage industry, peasants managed to get hold of over half of all the land on sale – even if this still left most holding unsustainable plots of a hectare or less, and needing other work to survive.

Compared to the lightning strikes of twentieth-century socialist land confiscations, these changes might seem limited, but compared to the glacial pace of multi-generational property accumulation in the Old Regime, they were indisputably revolutionary. Peasants now held these lands as unchallenged freeholders, not as feudal vassals, and resisted attempts to put their interests below those of landlords or 'improvers'. A further fundamental revolutionary legal change, imposing the right of all children to inherit equal shares of property, encouraged peasants to continue building up their farms, and also to limit their families.

All these shifts together produced a dramatic change in the demography of France, unseen anywhere else in the same era. Average family size fell from around six to under four within a generation, and with it, life expectancy at birth rose from under thirty to almost forty, largely due to declining infant mortality. The number of children surviving into their teenage years rose from under half to almost two-thirds. The French peasantry, through its resistance, broke the terrible cycle of pre-modern mortality without succumbing – as for example the British working class did – to a mass experience of even worse urban industrial mortality in the first half of the next century.

Of course, France did industrialize, and an increasing proportion of its population would shift to the towns, and in many cases experience gross exploitation and appalling conditions there. But the rural population continued to rise, peaking in absolute numbers in the 1840s, and remained almost half of the overall population as late as 1900. For advocates of industrialization, and of national grandeur, this situation would come to be seen as a problem in itself. By 1900, the idea that France was losing a 'Darwinian' population battle with Germany because of its low birth rate was widespread, and the terrible casualties of the First World War continued to make this an anxiety in the decades that followed.

But the independence of the French peasantry at the same time became a marker of the very nature of French republicanism, once various other experiments with monarchy and empire had been disposed of. At no point could it be said that farming was an easy life, but under the conditions created by the peasant resistance of the 1790s, it was a life more free, and more equal, than that enjoyed by almost anyone else among the working peoples of the world.

For much of the last two centuries, the lure of the spectacular divisions that erupted in France after 1789 has captured historical and political attention. Competing claims over the virtues or evils of the clergy and the nobility, the heady drama of crowd protests, the fiery rhetoric of Jacobins and 'terrorists', the siren call of national defence, and the mysterious yet apparently vital question of class identities in all this, have raged for decades. Within the conflicts of the 1790s, later generations have chosen to see the seeds of divisions that trouble their own times, whenever they may be, and inspiration for beliefs about how they might be solved.

But, obscured by the sound and fury of those years – years which, as any robust account shows, ended with the vicious implosion of every side's hopes – there remains the story of a real revolution in ordinary people's understanding of who they were. Ten years almost to the day after Arthur Young had met his nameless, weary, downtrodden peasant woman, hoping for someone else to do something for her, in July 1799 another peasant woman posted a blunt note on the severed stump of a republican 'tree of liberty' in the village of Villethierry in the Yonne.

Signing herself 'Suzanne the Fearless', and opening boldly 'Wake up people of France', she raged against the 'despotic' republican administration that forced Catholic worship behind closed doors and forbade Sunday celebrations, making a mockery of their assertions that 'you are free and sovereign' while 'enchained' by such restrictions – 'After this, are we sovereign? Isn't this playing with the people?'[55] Suzanne, of course, would be on the wrong side in any conventional progressive account of revolutionary radicalism, and as things stood her female descendants would have to wait more than 140 years for the right to take an active part in political life as voters alongside their menfolk. But there she was, at the close of the eighteenth century, demanding her freedoms as a member of the sovereign people, for what she wanted, not what some lawyer told her she ought to want, or some nobleman told her she could not have.

History is too often the story of competing efforts to trample the common people, and to cram their lives and dreams into predetermined moulds of continuity or change. But it is also the story of their fight not to be trampled, then, now and in the future. And the story of the French Revolution is a great example of how that fight, doggedly, painfully, can succeed.

Notes on Further Reading

My own previous books cover all the issues treated here in more detail:
The French Revolution and the People (London, 2004).
The Terror: Civil War in the French Revolution (London, 2005).
1789: The Threshold of the Modern Age (London, 2008).

Peter M. Jones, *The Peasantry in the French Revolution* (Cambridge, 1988) is a landmark of an earlier generation, and complemented by his close-up study, *Liberty and Locality in Revolutionary France: Six Villages Compared, 1760–1820* (Cambridge, 2003).

Peter McPhee, *Living the French Revolution, 1789–1799* (Basingstoke, 2006) is an eloquent overview of popular lives, and his *Liberty or Death: The French Revolution* (New Haven, 2016) is a swirling, riveting in-depth narrative of the Revolution as a whole.

David Andress (ed.), *The Oxford Handbook of the French Revolution* (Oxford, 2015), and Peter McPhee (ed.), *A Companion to the French Revolution* (Oxford, 2013) include between them over sixty individual essays covering every aspect of the period.

Notes

1   THE PEASANTS' WORLD

1   See http://www.econlib.org/library/YPDBooks/Young/yngTF4.html#Chapter 4, paragraph 4.46.

2   See http://historien.geographe.free.fr/cdrouffy-en-champagne.pdf.

3   Charles Etienne, ed., *Cahiers de doléances des bailliages des généralités de Metz et de Nancy pour les Etats généraux de 1789. Première série, Département de Meurthe-et-Moselle. 2, Cahiers du bailliage de Dieuze* (Nancy, 1912), p. 3.

2   THE PEASANTS' VOICE

4   Jill Walshaw, *A Show of Hands for the Republic: Opinion, Information, and Repression in Eighteenth-Century Rural France* (Woodbridge, 2014), pp. 89–91.

5   Pierre-Yves Beaurepaire, 'The View from Below: the 1789 *cahiers de doléances*', in D. Andress, ed., *The Oxford Handbook of the French Revolution* (Oxford, 2015), pp. 149–63; pp. 157, 158.

6   David Andress, *French Society in Revolution, 1789–1799* (Manchester, 1999), p. 168.

7   Beaurepaire, 'View from Below', p. 155.

8   Andress, *French Society*, p. 168.

9   Beaurepaire, 'View from Below', p. 160.

10 David Andress, *The French Revolution and the People* (London, 2004), p. 94.

11 Ibid., p. 102.

---

3   CRISIS AND REVOLUTION

12 David Andress, *1789: The Threshold of the Modern Age* (London, 2008), p. 313.

13 Ibid., p. 314.

14 See the full text translated in Keith Michael Baker, ed., *Readings in Western Civilisation, 7, the Old Regime and the French Revolution* (Chicago, 1987), pp. 228–31.

15 Baker, *Readings*, pp. 227–8.

16 Ibid., pp. 238–9.

---

4   FAILURES AND BETRAYALS

17 Andress, *French Revolution*, p. 125.

18 Walshaw, *Show of Hands*, p. 95.

19 Andress, *French Society*, p. 174.

20 Laura Mason and Tracy Rizzo, *The French Revolution: A Document Collection* (Boston, 1999), p. 129.

21 Peter Jones, *The Peasantry in the French Revolution* (Cambridge, 1988), p. 104.

22 Andress, *French Society*, p. 175.

23 Walshaw, *Show of Hands*, p. 146.

24 Andress, *French Revolution*, p. 136.

25 Ibid., p. 138.

26 Peter McPhee, *Liberty or Death: the French Revolution* (New Haven, 2016), p. 177.

---

5   SLIDING TO DISASTER

27 Andress, *French Revolution*, p. 141.

28 Walshaw, *Show of Hands*, p. 148.

29 David Andress, *Massacre at the Champ de Mars* (Woodbridge, 2000), p. 105.

---

6   TREASON

30 Timothy Tackett, *When the King Took Flight* (Cambridge, MA, 2003), pp. 8, 22–3.

31 Andress, *French Revolution*, pp. 169–70.

32 Ibid., p. 170.

---

7   WAR, MASSACRE AND TERROR

33 Andress, *French Revolution*, p. 181.

---

8   THE REPUBLIC AND THE PEOPLE

34 Andress, *French Revolution*, p. 192.

35 Walshaw, *Show of Hands*, p. 149.

36 McPhee, *Liberty*, p. 183.

37 David Andress, *The Terror: Civil War in the French Revolution* (London, 2004), p. 279.

38 Andress, *French Revolution*, p. 219.

39 Ibid., p. 220.

40 McPhee, *Liberty*, pp. 202–3.

41 Andress, *Terror*, pp. 278–9.

42 Ibid., p. 219.

43 Andress, *French Revolution*, p. 222.

---

9   SLAUGHTER AND REACTION

44 Andress, *French Revolution*, p. 224.

45 Andress, *Terror*, p. 236.

46 Ibid., p. 237.

47 Jill Maciak Walshaw, 'News and Networks: The Communication of Political Information in the Eighteenth-Century French Countryside', unpublished DPhil thesis, University of York, 2003, p. 152.

48 Alan Forrest, *Soldiers of the French Revolution* (Durham, NC, 1990), p. 160.

49 Ibid., p. 157.

10 MOVING ON, LOOKING BACK

50 Peter M. Jones, *Liberty and Locality in Revolutionary France: Six Villages Compared, 1760–1820* (Cambridge, 2003), pp. 164–6, 189–90.

51 Ibid., pp. 167–8.

52 Ibid., pp. 169–71.

53 McPhee, *Liberty*, p. 315.

54 D. M. G. Sutherland, *Murder in Aubagne: Lynching, Law, and Justice during the French Revolution* (Cambridge, 2009).

EPILOGUE: A FINAL RECKONING

55 Andress, *French Revolution*, p. 257.

Index

.